Sensational
Slow Cooker
Gourmet

Chunky Black Bean Chili

Sensational
Slow Cooker
Gourmet

Judith Finlayson

Robert
ROSE

For complete cataloguing information, see page 136.

Disclaimer
The recipes in this book have been carefully tested by our kitchen and our tasters. To the best of our knowledge, they are safe and nutritious for ordinary use and users. For those people with food or other allergies, or who have special food requirements or health issues, please read the suggested contents of each recipe carefully and determine whether or not they may create a problem for you. All recipes are used at the risk of the consumer.

We cannot be responsible for any hazards, loss or damage that may occur as a result of any recipe use.

For those with special needs, allergies, requirements or health problems, in the event of any doubt, please contact your medical adviser prior to the use of any recipe.

Design and Production: PageWave Graphics Inc.
Editor: Sue Sumeraj
Recipe Tester: Jennifer MacKenzie
Proofreader: Sheila Wawanash
Indexer: Gillian Watts
Photography: Colin Erricson (except pages 25, 45, 89 and 91 by Mark T. Shapiro)
Food Styling: Kathryn Robertson and Kate Bush
Prop Styling: Charlene Erricson

Cover image: Barley Jambalaya (page 98)

We acknowledge the financial support of the Government of Canada through the Book Publishing Industry Development Program (BPIDP) for our publishing activities.

Published by Robert Rose Inc.

120 Eglinton Avenue East, Suite 800, Toronto, Ontario, Canada M4P 1E2
Tel: (416) 322-6552 Fax: (416) 322-6936

Printed and bound in Canada
1 2 3 4 5 6 7 8 9 TCP 16 15 14 13 12 11 10 09 08

To Meredith

Contents

Using Your Slow Cooker

An Effective Time Manager

In addition to producing great-tasting food, a slow cooker is an extremely effective time-management tool. Where appropriate, I've included Make Ahead instructions that explain how to prepare a substantial amount of a recipe prior to cooking it, which enables you to be in the kitchen when it fits your schedule. (Some dishes and ingredients can't be assembled ahead of time for food safety or quality reasons.) Once the ingredients have been assembled in the stoneware and the appliance is turned on, you can forget about it. The slow cooker performs unattended while you carry on with your workaday life. You can be away from the kitchen all day and return to a hot, delicious meal.

Maximize Slow Cooker Convenience

To get the most out of your slow cooker:

- Use Make Ahead instructions to partially prepare a dish up to 2 days prior to cooking.
- Do any additional chopping and slicing the night before you intend to cook to keep work to a minimum when it is less convenient.
- Cook a recipe overnight and refrigerate until ready to serve.

A Low-Tech Appliance

Slow cookers are amazingly low tech. The appliance usually consists of a metal casing and a stoneware insert with a tight-fitting lid. For convenience, you should be able to remove the insert from the metal casing. This makes it easier to clean and increases its versatility, not only as a vessel for refrigerating some dishes that have been prepared to the Make Ahead stage but also as a serving dish. The casing contains the heat source, electrical coils that usually surround the stoneware insert. These coils do their work on the energy it takes to power a 100-watt light bulb.

Greek Bean Sauce with Feta

Because the slow cooker operates on such a small amount of energy, you can safely leave it turned on while you are away from home. However, if you've assembled the dish in the stoneware and refrigerated it overnight (appropriate for some dishes), do not turn the slow cooker on before dropping the stoneware into the casing. The dramatic temperature change could crack the stoneware.

Slow Cooker Basics

Slow cookers are generally round or oval in shape and range in size from 1 to 7 quarts. The small round ones are ideal for dips and fondues, as well as some soups, main courses and desserts. The larger sizes, usually oval in shape, are necessary to cook big-batch dishes and those that need to be cooked in a dish or pan that fits into the stoneware.

Because I use my slow cookers a lot for entertaining, I feel there is a benefit to having two: a smaller (3- to 4-quart size) one, which is ideal for preparing dips, roasting nuts or making recipes with smaller yields, and a larger (6-quart) oval one, which I use most of the time to cook recipes with large yields as well as for those calling for a baking dish or pan, which is set inside the stoneware. Once you begin using your slow cooker, you will get a sense of what your own needs are.

Some manufacturers sell a "slow cooker" that is actually a multi-cooker. These have a heating element at the bottom and, in my experience, they cook faster than traditional slow cookers. Also, since the heat source is at the bottom, during the long cooking time it is possible that the food will scorch unless it is stirred.

Your slow cooker should come with a booklet that explains how to use the appliance. I recommend that you read this carefully and/or visit the manufacturer's website for specific information on the model you purchased. I've used a variety of slow cookers and have found that cooking times can vary substantially from one to another.

Although it may not seem particularly helpful if you're just starting out, the only firm advice I can give is: Know your slow cooker. After trying a few of these recipes, you will get a sense of whether your slow cooker is faster or slower than the ones I use and you will be able to adjust the cooking times accordingly.

Other variables that can affect cooking time are extreme humidity, power fluctuations and high altitudes. Be extra vigilant if any of these circumstances affect you.

Cooking Great-Tasting Food

The slow cooker's less-is-better approach is, in many ways, the secret of its success. The appliance does its work by cooking foods very slowly — from about 200°F (100°C) on the Low setting to 300°F (150°C) on High. This slow, moist cooking environment (remember the tight-fitting lid) enables the appliance to produce mouth-watering pot roasts, briskets, chilies and many other kinds of soups and stews. It also helps to ensure success with delicate puddings and custards, among other dishes. In fact, I'm so pleased with the slow cooker's strengths that there are many dishes I wouldn't cook any other way — for instance, pot roast, beef brisket or short ribs, chilies and many kinds of stew. I also love to make cheesecakes in my slow cooker because they emerge from this damp cocoon perfectly cooked every time. They don't dry out or crack, which happens all too easily in the oven.

Easy Vegetable Chili

Slow Cooker Tips

Some benefits of long slow cooking:

- breaks down the tough connective tissue of less tender cuts of meat;
- allows the seasoning in complex sauces to intermingle without scorching;
- makes succulent chilies and stews that don't dry out or stick to the bottom of the pot;
- ensures success with delicate dishes such as puddings and custards.

Understanding Your Slow Cooker

Like all appliances, the slow cooker has its unique way of doing things and, as a result, you need to understand how it works and adapt your cooking style accordingly. When friends learned I was writing a slow cooker cookbook, many had a similar response: "Oh, you mean that appliance that allows you to throw the ingredients in and return to a home-cooked meal!"

"Well, sort of," was my response. Over the years, I've learned to think of my slow cooker as an indispensable helpmate, and I can hardly imagine living without its assistance. But I also know that it can't work miracles. Off the top of my head, I can't think of any great dish that results when ingredients are merely "thrown together." Success in the slow cooker, like success in the oven or on top of the stove, depends upon using proper cooking techniques. The slow cooker saves you time because it allows you to forget about the food once it is in the stoneware. But you still must pay attention to the advance preparation. Here are a few tips that will help to ensure slow cooker success.

Brown Meat and Soften Vegetables

Although it requires an extra pan, I am committed to browning most meats and softening vegetables before adding them to the slow cooker. In my experience, this is not the most time-consuming part of preparing a slow cooker dish — it usually takes longer to peel and chop the vegetables, which you have to do anyway. But it dramatically improves the quality of the dish for two reasons.

Not only does browning add color, but it also begins the process of caramelization, which breaks down the natural sugars in foods and releases their flavor. It also extracts the fat-soluble components of foods, which further enriches the taste. Moreover, tossing herbs and spices with the softened vegetables helps to produce a sauce in which the flavors are better integrated than they would have been if this step had been skipped.

Reduce the Quantity of Liquid

As you use your slow cooker, one of the first things you will notice is that it generates liquid. Because slow cookers cook at a low heat, tightly covered, liquid doesn't evaporate as it does in the oven or on top of the stove. As a result, food made from traditional recipes will be watery. So the second rule of successful slow cooking is to reduce the amount of liquid. Because you don't want to reduce the flavor, I prefer to cook with stock rather than water.

Cut Root Vegetables into Thin Slices or Small Pieces

Perhaps surprisingly, root vegetables — carrots, parsnips and particularly potatoes — cook even more slowly than meat in the slow cooker. As a result, root vegetables should be thinly sliced or cut into small pieces no larger than 1-inch (2.5 cm) cubes.

Pay Attention to Cooking Temperature

To achieve maximum results, less tender cuts of meat should be cooked as slowly as possible at the Low setting. Expect to cook whole cuts of meat such as roasts for 10 hours on Low and give brisket 12 hours on Low to become truly succulent. If you're short of time and at home during the day, cook whole cuts of meat on High for 1 to 2 hours before switching the temperature to Low. As noted in Food Safety (see page 18) if adding cold ingredients, particularly large cuts of meat, to the slow cooker, set on High for an hour before lowering the temperature.

Many desserts, such as those containing milk, cream or some leavening agents, need to be cooked on High. In these recipes, a Low setting is not suggested as an option. For recipes that aren't dependent upon cooking at a particular temperature, the rule of thumb is that 1 hour of cooking on High equals 2 to $2\frac{1}{2}$ hours on Low.

Don't Overcook

Although slow cooking reduces your chances of overcooking food, it is still not a "one size fits all" solution to meal preparation. If you want your slow cooker to cook pork chops or chicken while you are away, you should plan your day carefully. It is very easy to overcook poultry, which shouldn't require more than 6 hours on Low. If cooking white meat, which dries out easily, I recommend leaving the skin on, which helps to maintain precious moisture and flavor. Remove the skin when serving, if desired. Because legs and thighs stand up well in the slow cooker, I remove the skin before cooking to reduce the fat content in the sauce.

Use Ingredients Appropriately

Some ingredients do not respond well to long slow cooking and should be added during the last 30 minutes of cooking, after the temperature has been increased to High. These include: peas, leafy greens, seafood, milk and cream (which will curdle if cooked too long). I love to cook with peppers, but I've learned that most become bitter if cooked for too long. The solution to this problem is to add peppers to recipes during the last 30 minutes of cooking. All the recipes in this book address these concerns in the instructions.

Whole Leaf Herbs and Whole Spices

For best results use whole rather than ground herbs and spices in the slow cooker. Whole spices, such as cinnamon sticks, and whole leaf herbs, such as dried thyme and oregano leaves, release their flavors slowly throughout the long cooking period, unlike ground spices and herbs, which tend to lose flavor during slow cooking. If you're using fresh herbs, finely chop them and add during the last hour of cooking unless you include the whole stem (this works best with thyme and rosemary).

I recommend the use of cracked black peppercorns rather than ground pepper in most of my recipes because they release flavor slowly during the long cooking process. Cracked pepper can be purchased in the spice sections of supermarkets, but I like to make my own in a mortar with a pestle. A rolling pin or even a heavy can on its side will also break up the peppercorns for use in slow-cooked dishes. If you prefer to use ground black pepper, use one-quarter to one-half the amount of cracked black peppercorns called for in the recipe.

Using Dishes and Pans in the Slow Cooker

Some dishes, notably puddings and custards, need to be cooked in an extra dish, which is placed in the slow cooker stoneware. Not only will you need a large oval slow cooker for this purpose, finding a dish or pan that fits into the stoneware can be a challenge. I've found that standard 7-inch (17.5 cm) square, 4-cup (1 L) and 6-cup (1.5 L) ovenproof baking dishes or soufflé dishes are the best all-round dishes for this purpose and I've used them to cook most of the custard-like recipes in this book. A 7-inch (17.5 cm) springform pan, which fits into a large oval slow cooker, is also a useful purchase for making cheesecakes.

Before you decide to make a recipe requiring a baking dish, ensure that you have a container that will fit into your stoneware. I've noted the size and dimensions of the containers used in all relevant recipes. Be aware that varying the size and shape of the dish is likely to affect cooking times.

Moroccan-Spiced Beef with Couscous

Food Safety

Food Safety in the Slow Cooker

Because it cooks at a very low temperature for long periods of time, cooking with a slow cooker requires a bit more vigilance about food safety than does cooking at higher temperatures. The slow cooker needs to strike a delicate balance between cooking slowly enough that it doesn't require your attention and fast enough to ensure that food reaches temperatures that are appropriate to inhibit bacterial growth. Bacteria grow rapidly at temperatures higher than 40°F (4°C) and lower than 140°F (60°C). Once the temperature reaches 165°F (74°C) bacteria are killed. That's why it is so important to leave the lid on when you're slow cooking, particularly during the early stages. This helps to ensure that bacteria-killing temperatures are reached in the appropriate amount of time.

Slow cooker manufacturers have designed the appliance to ensure that bacterial growth is not a concern. So long as the lid is left on and the food is cooked for the appropriate length of time, that temperature will be reached quickly enough to ensure food safety. Unless you have made part of the recipe ahead and refrigerated it, most of the ingredients in my recipes are warm when added to the slow cooker (the meat has been browned and the sauce has been thickened on the stovetop), which adds a cushion of comfort to any potential concerns about food safety.

The following tips will help to ensure that utmost food safety standards are met:

- Keep food refrigerated until you are ready to cook. Bacteria multiply quickly at room temperature. Do not allow ingredients to rise to room temperature before cooking.
- Do not partially cook meat or poultry and refrigerate for subsequent cooking. If you're browning meat before adding it to the slow cooker, do so just before placing it in the slow cooker. When cooking meat try to get it to a high temperature as quickly as possible.

- If cooking a large cut of meat, such as a pot roast, which has been added to the stoneware without being browned, set the temperature at High for at least an hour to accelerate the cooking process.
- If preparing ingredients in advance of cooking, refrigerate precooked meat, such as ground beef or sausage, and vegetables in separate containers and assemble when ready to cook.
- Pay attention to the Make Ahead instructions for those recipes that can be partially prepared in advance of cooking because they have been developed to address food safety issues.
- Do not put frozen meat, fish or poultry into a slow cooker. Unless otherwise instructed, thaw frozen food before adding to the slow cooker. Frozen fruits and vegetables should usually be thawed under cold running water to separate before being added to recipes.
- Don't lift the lid while food is cooking. Each time the lid is removed it takes approximately 20 minutes to recover the lost heat. This increases the time it takes for the food to reach the "safe zone."
- If you are away and the power goes out, discard the food if it has not finished cooking. If the food has cooked completely, it should be safe for up to 2 hours.
- Refrigerate leftovers as quickly as possible.
- Do not reheat food in the slow cooker.

Testing for Safety

If you are concerned that your slow cooker isn't cooking quickly enough to ensure food safety, try this simple test. Fill the stoneware insert with 8 cups (2 L) of cold water. Set temperature to Low for 8 hours. Using an accurate thermometer, and checking quickly because the temperature drops when the lid is removed, check to ensure that the temperature is 185°F (85°C). If it has not reached that temperature, it's not heating food fast enough to avoid food safety problems. If the temperature is significantly higher than that, the appliance is not cooking slowly enough to be used as a slow cooker.

Blackberry Peach Cobbler

Leftovers

Cooked food can be kept warm in the slow cooker for up to 2 hours. At that point it should be transferred to small containers so it cools as rapidly as possible and refrigerated or frozen. Because the appliance heats up so slowly, food should never be reheated in a slow cooker.

Soups

Classic French Onion Soup

On a chilly day, there's nothing more appetizing than a bowl of steaming onion soup, bubbling away under a blanket of browned cheese. Normally, caramelizing the onions for this masterpiece is a laborious process that can easily involve an hour of almost constant stirring. Fortunately, your slow cooker can now do most of this tiresome work for you.   **Serves 6**

Vegetarian Friendly

10	onions, thinly sliced on the vertical	10
2 tbsp	melted butter	25 mL
1 tbsp	granulated sugar	15 mL
8 cups	Enhanced Vegetable Stock (see variation, page 134) or good-quality beef stock (see tip)	2 L
2 tbsp	brandy or cognac	25 mL
1 tsp	salt	5 mL
1 tsp	cracked black peppercorns	5 mL
12	slices baguette, about ½ inch (1 cm) thick	12
2 cups	shredded Swiss or Gruyère cheese	500 mL

- Works best in a large (minimum 5-quart) slow cooker
- 6 ovenproof soup bowls

1. In slow cooker stoneware, combine onions and butter. Cover and cook on High for 3 hours, stirring twice.

2. Add sugar and stir well. Place two clean tea towels, each folded in half (so you will have four layers), over top of stoneware, to absorb the moisture. Cover and cook on High for 4 hours, stirring two or three times to ensure that onions are browning evenly, replacing towels each time.

3. Add stock, brandy, salt and pepper. Remove towels, cover and cook on High for 2 hours. Preheat broiler.

4. Ladle soup into ovenproof bowls. Place 2 baguette slices in each bowl. Sprinkle liberally with cheese and broil until top is bubbly and brown, for 2 to 3 minutes. Serve immediately.

> **TIP**
> Since it's important that the stock for this soup be top-quality, I recommend using homemade stock or, if you're not vegetarian, enhancing canned beef stock. To improve 8 cups (2 L) canned beef stock, combine in a large saucepan over medium heat with 2 carrots, peeled and coarsely chopped, 1 tsp (5 mL) celery seed, 1 tsp (5 mL) cracked black peppercorns, ½ tsp (2 mL) dried thyme, 4 sprigs fresh parsley, 1 bay leaf and 1 cup (250 mL) dry white wine. Bring to a boil. Reduce heat to low, cover and simmer for 30 minutes, then strain and discard solids.

Creamy Onion Soup with Kale

There is no cream in this delicious soup — unless you decide to drizzle a bit over individual servings. The creaminess is achieved with the addition of potatoes, which are puréed into the soup, providing it with a velvety texture.

Serves 6

Vegan Friendly

4	slices bacon (optional, see tips)	4
4	onions, thinly sliced	4
2	cloves garlic, minced	2
4	whole allspice	4
1	bay leaf	1
1 tsp	grated lemon zest	5 mL
½ tsp	cracked black peppercorns	2 mL
4 cups	vegetable or chicken stock (store-bought or see recipes, pages 134 and 135)	1 L
3	potatoes, peeled and diced	3
4 cups	chopped kale	1 L
1 tsp	paprika (see tips), dissolved in 2 tbsp (25 mL) freshly squeezed lemon juice	5 mL

MAKE AHEAD

Complete Steps 1 and 2. Cover and refrigerate for up to 2 days. When you're ready to cook, continue with the recipe.

- **Works best in a large (minimum 5-quart) slow cooker**

1. In a skillet, cook bacon (if using) over medium–high heat until crisp. Drain on a paper towel and crumble. Cover and refrigerate until ready to use. Drain off all but 2 tbsp (25 mL) fat from pan.

2. Reduce heat to medium. Add onions to pan and cook, stirring, until softened, about 5 minutes. Add garlic, allspice, bay leaf, lemon zest and peppercorns; cook, stirring, for 1 minute. Transfer to slow cooker stoneware.

3. Stir in stock and potatoes. Cover and cook on Low for 8 hours or on High for 4 hours, until potatoes are tender. Discard allspice and bay leaf. Stir in kale, paprika solution and reserved bacon (if using). Cover and cook on High for 20 minutes, until kale is tender.

4. Working in batches, purée soup in a food processor or blender. (You can also do this in the stoneware, using an immersion blender.) Serve immediately.

TIPS

If you are making this soup for vegetarians, omit the bacon and heat 1 tbsp (15 mL) vegetable oil in a skillet over medium heat for 30 seconds. Add the onions and continue with the recipe.

You can use any kind of paprika in this recipe: regular; hot, which produces a nicely peppery version; or smoked, which adds a delicious note of smokiness to the soup. If you have regular paprika and would like a bit a heat, dissolve ¼ tsp (1 mL) cayenne pepper in the lemon juice along with the paprika.

Beet Soup with Lemongrass and Lime

This Thai-inspired soup, which is served cold, is elegant and refreshing. Its jewel-like appearance and intriguing flavors make it a perfect prelude to any meal. I especially like to serve it at summer dinners in the garden.

Serves 6

Vegan Friendly

1 tbsp	olive oil or extra-virgin coconut oil (see tip)	15 mL
1	onion, chopped	1
4	cloves garlic, minced	4
2	stalks lemongrass, trimmed, smashed and cut in half crosswise	2
2 tbsp	minced gingerroot	25 mL
2 tsp	cracked black peppercorns	10 mL
6 cups	vegetable stock (store-bought or see recipe, page 134)	1.5 L
6	beets (about 2½ lbs/ 1.25 kg), peeled and chopped	6
1	red bell pepper, diced	1
1	long red chile pepper, seeded and diced (optional)	1
	Grated zest and juice of 1 lime	
	Salt (optional)	
	Coconut cream (optional)	
	Finely chopped fresh cilantro	

MAKE AHEAD

Ideally, make this soup the day before you intend to serve it so it can chill overnight in the refrigerator.

• Works in slow cookers from 3½ to 6 quarts

1. In a skillet, heat oil over medium heat for 30 seconds. Add onion and cook, stirring, until softened, about 3 minutes. Add garlic, lemongrass, ginger and peppercorns; cook, stirring, for 1 minute. Transfer to slow cooker stoneware.

2. Stir in stock and beets. Cover and cook on Low for 8 hours or on High for 4 hours, until beets are tender. Add red pepper and chile pepper (if using). Cover and cook on High for 30 minutes, until peppers are tender. Discard lemongrass.

3. Working in batches, purée soup in a food processor or blender. (You can also do this in the stoneware, using an immersion blender.) Transfer to a large bowl and stir in lime zest and juice. Season to taste with salt (if using). Cover and refrigerate until thoroughly chilled, preferably overnight.

4. Ladle into bowls, drizzle with coconut cream (if using) and garnish with cilantro.

TIP

I often use coconut oil when making this soup because its pleasantly nutty taste complements the Thai flavors.

Butternut Apple Soup with Swiss Cheese

Topped with melted cheese, this creamy and delicious soup makes a light main course, accompanied by a green salad. It can also be served as a starter to a more substantial meal.

Serves 6 to 8

Vegetarian Friendly

1 tbsp	olive oil	15 mL
2	onions, chopped	2
4	cloves garlic, minced	4
2 tsp	dried rosemary, crumbled (or 1 tbsp/ 15 mL chopped fresh)	10 mL
½ tsp	cracked black peppercorns	2 mL
5 cups	vegetable or chicken stock (store-bought or see recipes, pages 134 and 135)	1.25 L
2	tart apples (such as Granny Smith), peeled and coarsely chopped	2
1	butternut squash (about 2½ lbs/1.25 kg), cut into 1-inch (2.5 cm) cubes	1
	Salt (optional)	
1 cup	shredded Swiss cheese	250 mL
½ cup	finely chopped walnuts (optional)	125 mL

MAKE AHEAD

Complete Step 1. Cover and refrigerate for up to 2 days. When you're ready to cook, continue with the recipe.

- Works best in a large (minimum 5-quart) slow cooker

1. In a skillet, heat oil over medium heat for 30 seconds. Add onions and cook, stirring, until softened, about 3 minutes. Add garlic, rosemary and peppercorns; cook, stirring, for 1 minute. Transfer to slow cooker stoneware.

2. Stir in stock, apples and squash. Cover and cook on Low for 8 hours or on High for 4 hours, until squash is tender. Preheat broiler.

3. Working in batches, purée soup in a food processor or blender. (You can also do this in the stoneware, using an immersion blender.) Season to taste with salt (if using).

4. Ladle into ovenproof bowls. Sprinkle with cheese and broil until cheese melts, about 2 minutes. (You can also do this in batches in a microwave oven on High, about 1 minute per batch.) Sprinkle with walnuts (if using). Serve immediately.

Vichyssoise with Celery Root and Watercress

This refreshing soup is delicious and easy to make, and can be a prelude to the most sophisticated meal. More nutritious than traditional vichyssoise, it has a pleasing nutty flavor that may be enhanced with a garnish of chopped toasted walnuts. In the summer, I aim to have leftovers in the refrigerator and treat myself to a small bowl for a yummy afternoon snack. **Serves 6 to 8**

Vegan Friendly

1 tbsp	olive oil	15 mL
3	leeks, white and light green parts only, cleaned (see tips) and coarsely chopped	3
2	cloves garlic, minced	2
½ tsp	cracked black peppercorns	2 mL
6 cups	vegetable or chicken stock (store-bought or see recipes, pages 134 and 135)	1.5 L
1	large celery root (celeriac), peeled and sliced	1
2	bunches (each about 4 oz/125 g) watercress, tough parts of the stems removed	2
	Salt (optional)	
½ cup	whipping (35%) cream or soy milk	125 mL
	Toasted chopped walnuts (optional)	
	Watercress sprigs (optional)	

MAKE AHEAD

Complete Step 1. Cover and refrigerate for up to 2 days. When you're ready to cook, continue with the recipe.

- **Works best in a large (minimum 5-quart) slow cooker**

1. In a skillet, heat oil over medium heat for 30 seconds. Add leeks and cook, stirring, until softened, about 5 minutes. Add garlic and peppercorns; cook, stirring, for 1 minute. Transfer to slow cooker stoneware.

2. Stir in stock and celery root. Cover and cook on Low for 6 hours or on High for 3 hours, until celery root is tender. Stir in watercress until wilted.

3. Working in batches, purée soup in a food processor or blender. (You can also do this in the stoneware, using an immersion blender.) Season to taste with salt (if using). Stir in cream. Cover and refrigerate until thoroughly chilled, about 4 hours (see tip, below).

4. Ladle into bowls and garnish with walnuts and/or watercress (if using).

TIPS

To clean leeks, fill a basin full of lukewarm water. Split the leeks in half lengthwise and submerge them in the water, swishing them around to remove all traces of dirt. Transfer to a colander and rinse thoroughly under cold water.

Since celery root oxidizes quickly on contact with air, be sure to use it as soon as you have peeled and chopped it, or toss it with 1 tbsp (15 mL) lemon juice to prevent discoloration.

To cool the soup more quickly, transfer it to a large bowl before refrigerating.

Harira

This traditional Moroccan soup, often made with lamb, is usually served during Ramadan at the end of a day of fasting. This vegetarian version is finished with a dollop of harissa, a spicy North African sauce, which adds flavor and punch. Served with whole-grain bread, harira makes a great light meal. A salad of shredded carrots topped with a sprinkling of currants adds color to the meal and complements the Middle Eastern flavors.

Serves 6

Vegan Friendly

1 tbsp	olive oil	15 mL
4	stalks celery, diced	4
2	onions, coarsely chopped	2
2	cloves garlic, minced	2
1 tbsp	ground turmeric	15 mL
1 tbsp	grated lemon zest	15 mL
½ tsp	cracked black peppercorns	2 mL
1	can (28 oz/796 mL) diced tomatoes, with juice	1
4 cups	vegetable or chicken stock (store-bought or see recipes, pages 134 and 135)	1 L
1 cup	dried red lentils, rinsed	250 mL
1	can (14 to 19 oz/398 to 540 mL) chickpeas, drained and rinsed (see tip)	1
½ cup	finely chopped fresh parsley	125 mL
	Harissa (see recipe, page 132)	

MAKE AHEAD

Complete Step 1. Cover and refrigerate for up to 2 days. When you're ready to cook, continue with the recipe.

- Works best in a large (minimum 5-quart) slow cooker

1. In a skillet, heat oil over medium heat for 30 seconds. Add celery and onions; cook, stirring, until celery is softened, about 5 minutes. Add garlic, turmeric, lemon zest and peppercorns; cook, stirring, for 1 minute. Add tomatoes with juice and bring to a boil. Transfer to slow cooker stoneware.

2. Stir in stock, lentils and chickpeas. Cover and cook on Low for 6 to 8 hours or on High for 3 to 4 hours, until mixture is hot and bubbly and lentils are tender. Stir in parsley.

3. Ladle into bowls and pass the harissa at the table.

TIP

If you prefer, you can use 1 cup (250 mL) dried chickpeas, soaked, cooked and drained (see Basic Beans, page 133), instead of the canned chickpeas.

Fennel-Scented Tomato and Wild Rice Soup

If, like me, you get cravings for tomatoes, this soup is for you. Made with fire-roasted tomatoes (see tip, below), it provides a real tomato hit. The fennel brings intriguing licorice flavor, and the wild rice adds texture to make this soup particularly enjoyable. **Serves 8 as a main course**

Vegan Friendly

1 tbsp	olive oil	15 mL
2	leeks, white part only with just a hint of green, cleaned and sliced (see tip, page 32)	2
1	bulb fennel, cored and thinly sliced on the vertical	1
3	cloves garlic, sliced	3
1 tsp	fennel seeds, toasted and ground (see tips)	5 mL
½ tsp	salt (optional)	2 mL
½ tsp	freshly ground black pepper	2 mL
1	can (28 oz/796 mL) crushed tomatoes	1
4 cups	vegetable or chicken stock (store-bought or see recipes, pages 134 and 135), divided	1 L
¾ cup	wild rice, rinsed and drained	175 mL
	Whipping (35%) cream (optional)	
	Finely chopped fresh parsley or fennel fronds	

MAKE AHEAD

Complete Steps 1 and 2, but do not add the rice and remaining stock. Cover and refrigerate for up to 2 days. When you're ready to cook, add the refrigerated mixture, wild rice and remaining stock to the stoneware. Continue with the recipe.

- Works best in a large (minimum 5-quart) slow cooker

1. In a large saucepan or stockpot, heat oil over medium heat for 30 seconds. Add leeks and fennel; cook, stirring, until softened, about 7 minutes. Add garlic, fennel seeds, salt (if using) and pepper; cook, stirring, for 1 minute. Stir in tomatoes and half the stock. Remove from heat.

2. Using an immersion blender, purée soup. (You can also do this in batches in a food processor, then return the soup to the pot.) Return to medium heat. Add the remaining stock and wild rice; bring to a boil. Transfer to slow cooker stoneware.

3. Cover and cook on Low for 8 hours or on High for 4 hours, until rice is tender and grains have begun to split.

4. Ladle into bowls, drizzle with cream (if using) and garnish with parsley.

TIPS

Toasting fennel seeds intensifies their flavor. To toast, stir fennel seeds in a dry skillet over medium heat until fragrant, about 3 minutes. Transfer to a mortar or spice grinder and grind.

To prepare fennel, before removing the core, chop off the top shoots (which resemble celery) and discard. If desired, save the feathery green fronds to use as a garnish. If the outer sections of the bulb seem old and dry, peel them with a vegetable peeler before using.

Whether you use salt, and the quantity, will depend on the sodium content of your stock.

For a slightly more intense tomato flavor, substitute 2 cans (each 14 oz/398 mL) fire-roasted tomatoes with juice for the crushed tomatoes.

Miso-Spiked Vegetable Soup with Barley

Here's a hearty vegetable soup that's the perfect antidote to a blustery day. The addition of miso adds robustness and a hint of complexity that is often lacking in simple vegetable soups. Serve this with your favorite sandwich for a delicious soup and sandwich meal. **Serves 6 as a main course**

Vegan Friendly

1 tbsp	olive oil	15 mL
4	carrots, peeled and diced	4
4	stalks celery, diced	4
2	onions, finely chopped	2
1 tsp	dried thyme	5 mL
½ tsp	cracked black peppercorns	2 mL
1 cup	barley (see tip), rinsed and drained	250 mL
7 cups	vegetable or chicken stock (store-bought or see recipes, pages 134 and 135)	1.75 L
2 cups	sliced green beans	500 mL
¼ cup	dark miso	50 mL
½ cup	finely chopped fresh parsley	125 mL
	Freshly grated Parmesan cheese (optional)	

VARIATION

Miso-Spiked Vegetable Soup with Wheat Berries

Substitute an equal quantity of wheat, spelt or Kamut berries for the barley.

MAKE AHEAD

Complete Step 1. Cover and refrigerate for up to 2 days. When you're ready to cook, continue with the recipe.

- **Works best in a large (minimum 5-quart) slow cooker**

1. In a skillet, heat oil over medium heat for 30 seconds. Add carrots, celery and onions; cook, stirring, until carrots are softened, about 7 minutes. Add thyme and peppercorns; cook, stirring, for 1 minute. Add barley and toss to coat. Add stock and bring to a boil. Transfer to slow cooker stoneware.

2. Cover and cook on Low for 8 hours or on High for 4 hours, until barley is tender. Add green beans and miso. Cover and cook on High until beans are tender, about 15 minutes. Stir in parsley.

3. Ladle into bowls and garnish with Parmesan (if using).

> **TIP**
> Use the variety of barley you prefer — pearled, pot or whole. Whole (also known as hulled) barley is the most nutritious form of the grain.

Fragrant Beef and Barley Soup with Chinese Mushrooms

Here's an updated version of a classic soup. The Chinese accents add intriguing flavors and give it a global spin without detracting from its traditional appeal. **Serves 6 as a main course**

8	dried shiitake mushrooms	8
3 cups	hot water	750 mL
1 tbsp	vegetable oil	15 mL
8 oz	stewing beef, trimmed, cut into bite-size pieces and patted dry	250 g
4	stalks celery, diced	4
2	onions, finely chopped	2
1 tbsp	minced garlic	15 mL
1 tbsp	minced gingerroot	15 mL
½ tsp	cracked black pepper	2 mL
½ tsp	Chinese five-spice powder (see tips)	2 mL
8 oz	fresh shiitake mushrooms, stems removed and caps sliced	250 g
⅔ cup	barley (see tips)	150 mL
4 cups	beef stock (see tips)	1 L
¼ cup	soy sauce	50 mL
	Finely chopped green onions (optional)	

VEGETARIAN ALTERNATIVE

Barley Soup with Chinese Mushrooms

Substitute 8 oz (250 g) portobello mushrooms, stemmed, gilled and chopped, for the stewing beef and an equal quantity of vegetable stock for the beef stock.

MAKE AHEAD

See page 44.

- Works best in a large (minimum 5-quart) slow cooker

1. In a bowl, combine dried mushrooms with hot water. Let stand for 30 minutes. Strain through a coffee filter or a sieve lined with a damp paper towel, reserving liquid. Remove stems. Pat mushrooms dry and chop finely. Set mushrooms and liquid aside separately.

2. In a skillet, heat oil over medium heat for 30 seconds. Add beef, celery, onions, and reserved mushrooms; cook, stirring, for 1 minute. Reduce heat to low, cover and cook until vegetables are softened, about 8 minutes. Add garlic, ginger, pepper and five-spice powder; cook, stirring, for 1 minute. Add fresh mushrooms and barley; toss to coat. Add stock and reserved mushroom soaking water; bring to a boil over high heat. Transfer to slow cooker stoneware.

3. Cover and cook on Low for 8 hours or on High for 4 hours, until barley is tender. Stir in soy sauce.

4. Ladle into bowls and garnish with green onions (if using).

TIPS

If you prefer a milder mushroom flavor, substitute 1 package (½ oz/14 g) dried wood ear mushrooms for the dried shiitakes.

Chinese five-spice powder is available in the spice section of well-stocked supermarkets or in Asian markets.

Use the variety of barley you prefer — pearled, pot or whole. Whole (also known as hulled) barley is the most nutritious form of the grain.

If desired, use 1 box (1 quart/900 mL) ready-to-use reduced-sodium beef stock for this quantity.

Southwestern Turkey Chowder

This soup is so good I can't wait to finish the celebratory turkey and get it started. I think it's the best way to use up leftover turkey and any leftover bits of long-cooking whole grains. If you're planning to eat lightly following the holiday, it makes a perfect dinner with the addition of salad.

Serves 6 to 8 as a main course

1 tbsp	olive oil	15 mL
4	stalks celery, diced	4
3	onions, finely chopped	3
4	cloves garlic, minced	4
1 tbsp	ground cumin (see tips)	15 mL
2 tsp	dried oregano	10 mL
½ tsp	cracked black peppercorns	2 mL
1½ cups	long-cooking whole grains (see tips), rinsed and drained	375 mL
9 cups	turkey stock (see variation, page 135)	2.25 L
1	can (28 oz/796 mL) diced tomatoes, with juice	1
2 to 3	dried ancho, guajillo or mild New Mexico chiles	2 to 3
2 cups	boiling water	500 mL
1 cup	loosely packed fresh cilantro leaves	250 mL
2 cups	diced cooked turkey	500 mL
2 cups	corn kernels, thawed if frozen	500 mL

VARIATION

Southwestern Chicken Chowder
Substitute chicken stock for the turkey stock and diced cooked chicken for the turkey.

MAKE AHEAD

Complete Step 1. Cover and refrigerate for up to 2 days. When you're ready to cook, continue with the recipe.

- **Works best in a large (minimum 5-quart) slow cooker**

1. In a stockpot, heat oil over medium heat for 30 seconds. Add celery and onions; cook, stirring, until softened, about 5 minutes. Add garlic, cumin, oregano and peppercorns; cook, stirring, for 1 minute. Add whole grains and toss to coat. Add stock and tomatoes with juice; bring to a boil. Transfer to slow cooker stoneware.

2. Cover and cook on Low for 8 hours or High for 4 hours, until grains are tender.

3. About an hour before recipe has finished cooking, combine dried chiles and boiling water in a heatproof bowl. Set aside for 30 minutes, weighing chiles down with a cup to ensure they remain submerged. Drain, discarding soaking liquid and stems, and coarsely chop chiles. Transfer to a blender and add cilantro and ½ cup (125 mL) stock from the chowder; purée.

4. Add chile mixture to stoneware, along with turkey and corn, and stir well. Cover and cook on High for 20 minutes, until corn is tender and flavors meld.

TIPS

For the best flavor, toast and grind whole cumin seeds rather than buying ground cumin. Simply stir seeds in a dry skillet over medium heat until fragrant, about 3 minutes. Immediately transfer to a spice grinder or mortar and grind.

Use any combination of long-cooking whole grains in this soup, such as barley, wheat, spelt or Kamut berries or brown, red or wild rice. All will be delicious. You can even use just one grain, if you prefer.

Manhattan Clam Chowder

Manhattan clam chowder is an appealing lighter alternative to traditional New England–style chowder.

Serves 4 as a main course or 6 as a starter

1 tbsp	vegetable oil	15 mL
4	slices bacon	4
2	onions, finely chopped	2
2	stalks celery, thinly sliced	2
2	carrots, peeled and diced	2
2	cloves garlic, minced	2
1 tsp	dried thyme	5 mL
½ tsp	cracked black peppercorns	2 mL
1 cup	dry white wine or water mixed with 2 tsp (10 mL) lemon juice	250 mL
1	can (28 oz/796 mL) diced tomatoes, with juice	1
1 cup	bottled clam juice	250 mL
1 cup	water	250 mL
2	potatoes, finely diced (see tips)	2
2½ lbs	clams, cleaned (see tips)	1.25 kg
1 cup	corn kernels, thawed if frozen	250 mL
	Finely chopped fresh parsley	

MAKE AHEAD

Complete Steps 1 and 2. Cover and refrigerate for up to 2 days. When ready to cook, continue with the recipe.

- Works in slow cookers from 3½ to 6 quarts

1. In a skillet, heat oil over medium-high heat for 30 seconds. Add bacon and cook until crisp. Drain on a paper towel and crumble. Cover and refrigerate until ready to use. Drain off all but 2 tbsp (25 mL) fat from pan.

2. Reduce heat to medium. Add onions, celery and carrots to pan and cook, stirring, until softened, about 7 minutes. Add garlic, thyme and peppercorns; cook, stirring, for 1 minute. Add wine, bring to a boil and cook until reduced by half, about 3 minutes. (If you are using water, add it with the tomatoes.) Add tomatoes with juice, clam juice and water; bring to a boil. Transfer to slow cooker stoneware.

3. Stir in potatoes. Cover and cook on Low for 8 hours or on High for 4 hours, until potatoes are tender.

4. Discard any clams that are open. In a large saucepan, over medium-high heat, bring ½ cup (125 mL) water to a rapid boil. Add clams, cover and cook, shaking the pot, until all the clams open. Discard any that do not open. Strain cooking liquid through a fine sieve. Using a fork, remove clam meat from shells.

5. Add clam meat and cooking liquid to slow cooker, along with corn and reserved bacon. Cover and cook on High for 15 minutes, until corn is tender and mixture is heated through.

6. Ladle into bowls and garnish liberally with parsley.

TIPS

Be sure to cut potatoes into fine dice. Otherwise, they will not be fully cooked in the slow cooker.

To clean clams, scrub thoroughly with a wire brush and soak in several changes of cold salted water.

Substitute 2 cans (each 5 oz/142 g) baby clams, drained and rinsed, for the fresh clams, if desired. Add ½ cup (125 mL) water along with the canned clams.

Beef, Pork and Lamb

Tailgaters' Favorite Stew

I can't imagine anything more appealing on a blustery day than a big serving of this ambrosial stew. It's great for potlucks and outdoor get-togethers because it's easily transportable and there is nothing to add.

Serves 6 to 8

6	slices bacon (about 4 oz/125 g)	6
¼ cup	all-purpose flour	50 mL
1 tsp	salt	5 mL
½ tsp	cracked black peppercorns	2 mL
¼ tsp	cayenne pepper	1 mL
2 lbs	stewing beef, trimmed, cut into 1-inch (2.5 cm) cubes and patted dry	1 kg
2	onions, finely chopped	2
2	stalks celery, diced	2
2	carrots, peeled and diced	2
4	cloves garlic, minced	4
2	bay leaves	2
½ tsp	freshly grated nutmeg	2 mL
	Grated zest and juice of 1 orange	
1½ cups	barley (see tips) rinsed and drained	375 mL
2 cups	beef stock	500 mL
1 cup	dry red wine	250 mL
1 cup	water	250 mL
1	can (5½ oz/156 mL) tomato paste	1

VARIATION

Substitute wheat, spelt or Kamut berries for the barley.

MAKE AHEAD

Complete Step 3, heating 1 tbsp (15 mL) oil in pan before softening the vegetables. Cover and refrigerate for up to 2 days. To cook, sauté the bacon and brown the beef. Combine with vegetable mixture and continue with Step 4.

- **Works best in a large (minimum 5-quart) slow cooker**

1. In a skillet, cook bacon over medium–high heat until crisp. Drain on a paper towel and crumble. Cover and refrigerate until ready to use. Drain off all but 2 tbsp (25 mL) fat from pan, reserving remainder.

2. On a plate, combine flour, salt, peppercorns and cayenne. Dredge beef in mixture until coated, discarding any excess. Add beef to pan, in batches, and cook, stirring, until lightly browned, about 4 minutes per batch, adding more bacon drippings between batches if necessary. Using a slotted spoon, transfer to slow cooker stoneware as completed.

3. Reduce heat to medium. Add onions, celery and carrots to pan and cook, stirring, until carrots are softened, about 7 minutes. Add garlic, bay leaves, nutmeg and orange zest; cook, stirring, for 1 minute. Add barley, stock, wine, water, tomato paste and orange juice; bring to a boil. Transfer to stoneware and stir well.

4. Cover and cook on Low for 8 hours or on High for 4 hours, until beef is tender. Discard bay leaves. Stir in reserved bacon.

TIPS

The orange zest and juice add wonderful depth to this stew.

Use the variety of barley you prefer — pearled, pot or whole. Whole (also known as hulled) barley is the most nutritious form of the grain.

Country Stew with Fennel

Full of character, this robust beef stew, which is rooted in French country cooking, is the perfect antidote to a bone-chilling night. Don't worry if you're not a fan of anchovies — they add depth to the sauce and their taste is negligible in the finished dish. I like to serve this over quinoa or whole wheat couscous, liberally garnished with parsley, but mashed potatoes work well too. **Serves 6**

½ tsp	fennel seeds	2 mL
1 tbsp	olive oil (approx.)	15 mL
1½ lbs	stewing beef, trimmed, cut into 1-inch (2.5 cm) cubes and patted dry	750 g
4	stalks celery, thinly sliced	4
2	onions, finely chopped	2
1	bulb fennel, cored and thinly sliced on the vertical	1
4	cloves garlic, minced	4
4	anchovy fillets, minced	4
1 tsp	dried thyme	5 mL
½ tsp	salt	2 mL
½ tsp	cracked black peppercorns	2 mL
1 tbsp	all-purpose flour	15 mL
1	can (28 oz/796 mL) tomatoes, with juice, coarsely chopped	1
2	bay leaves	2
½ cup	sliced pitted black olives	125 mL
	Fennel fronds	

MAKE AHEAD

Complete Step 1. Complete Step 3, heating 1 tbsp (15 mL) oil in pan before softening the vegetables. Cover and refrigerate for up to 2 days. When you're ready to cook, either brown the beef as outlined in Step 2 or add it to the stoneware without browning. Stir well and continue with Step 4.

- **Works best in a large (minimum 5-quart) slow cooker**

1. In a dry skillet over medium heat, toast fennel seeds, stirring, until fragrant, about 3 minutes. Immediately transfer to a mortar or a spice grinder and grind. (Or place the seeds on a cutting board and crush, using the bottom of a bottle or cup.) Set aside.

2. In the same skillet, heat oil over medium–high heat for 30 seconds. Add beef, in batches, and cook, stirring, until lightly browned, about 4 minutes per batch, adding a bit more oil between batches if necessary. Using a slotted spoon, transfer to slow cooker stoneware as completed.

3. Reduce heat to medium. Add celery, onions and sliced fennel to pan and cook, stirring, until celery is softened, about 5 minutes. Add garlic, anchovies, thyme, salt, peppercorns and reserved fennel seeds; cook, stirring, for 1 minute. Add flour and cook, stirring, for 1 minute. Add tomatoes with juice and bring to a boil. Cook, stirring, just until mixture begins to thicken, about 2 minutes. Stir in bay leaves. Transfer to stoneware and stir well.

4. Cover and cook on Low for 8 hours or on High for 4 hours, until beef is tender. Discard bay leaves. Stir in olives. Garnish with fennel fronds, if using.

> **TIP**
> To prepare fennel, before removing the core, chop off the top shoots (which resemble celery) and discard. If desired, save the feathery green fronds to use as a garnish. If the outer sections of the bulb seem old and dry, peel them with a vegetable peeler before using.

Moroccan-Spiced Beef with Couscous

Here's a stew that is every bit as delicious as it is unusual. I love the hint of sweetness provided by the parsnips and the way the spices combine to create the richly flavored broth. Accompanied by a bowl of steaming couscous, this makes a perfect meal for any occasion.   **Serves 6**

1 tbsp	vegetable oil (approx.)	15 mL
2 lbs	stewing beef, trimmed, cut into 1-inch (2.5 cm) cubes and patted dry	1 kg
4	each large carrots and parsnips (about 2 lbs/1 kg), peeled and chopped	4
2	onions, chopped	2
4	cloves garlic, minced	4
1	stick cinnamon, about 6 inches (15 cm) long	1
2 tbsp	cumin seeds, toasted and ground (see tip)	25 mL
2 tsp	coriander seeds, toasted and ground	10 mL
1 tsp	cracked black peppercorns	5 mL
2 tbsp	all-purpose flour	25 mL
1	can (28 oz/796 mL) diced tomatoes, drained	1
1 cup	beef stock	250 mL
½ cup	dry red wine	125 mL
1 tbsp	tomato paste	15 mL
	Salt	
½ tsp	cayenne pepper, dissolved in 1 tbsp (15 mL) freshly squeezed lemon juice	2 mL
	Finely chopped fresh parsley	
	Cooked couscous	

MAKE AHEAD

See page 72.

- Works best in a large (minimum 5-quart) slow cooker

1. In a skillet, heat oil over medium–high heat for 30 seconds. Add beef, in batches, and cook, stirring, until lightly browned, about 4 minutes per batch, adding a bit more oil between batches if necessary. Using a slotted spoon, transfer to slow cooker stoneware as completed.

2. Reduce heat to medium. Add carrots, parsnips and onions to pan and cook, stirring, until carrots are softened, about 7 minutes. Add garlic, cinnamon stick, cumin, coriander and peppercorns; cook, stirring, for 1 minute. Add flour and cook, stirring, for 1 minute. Add tomatoes, stock, wine and tomato paste; bring to a boil, stirring. Season to taste with salt. Transfer to stoneware and stir well.

3. Cover and cook on Low for 8 hours or on High for 4 hours, until beef is tender. Discard cinnamon stick. Stir in cayenne solution.

4. Ladle into bowls and garnish liberally with parsley. Serve with couscous.

> **TIP**
>
> Toasting the cumin and coriander seeds intensifies their flavor. Stir the seeds in a dry skillet over medium heat until fragrant, about 3 minutes. Transfer to a mortar or spice grinder and grind.
>
> You can use Israeli couscous (pictured here) — a larger and particularly succulent version of the product — or, for a nutritional boost, use whole wheat, spelt, Kamut or barley couscous. All are much more wholesome than couscous made from refined flour and are just as easy to prepare.

Carbonnade with Collards

Carbonnade, a stew made of beef, onions and beer, is a favorite dish in Belgium. It is hearty bistro food, often flavored with bacon and brown sugar. Although it is great comfort food, carbonnade can be a tad bland and extremely rich. I prefer this lighter version, with a hint of spice rather than sweetness and the addition of flavorful and nutrient-dense collard greens. Serve this over noodles or mashed potatoes for a meal that is destined to become a family favorite.

Serves 6

4 oz	chunk bacon, diced	125 g
2 lbs	stewing beef, trimmed, cut into 1-inch (2.5 cm) cubes and patted dry	1 kg
3	onions, thinly sliced on the vertical	3
4	cloves garlic, minced	4
1 tsp	dried thyme, crumbled	5 mL
1 tsp	salt	5 mL
1 tsp	cracked black peppercorns	5 mL
2 tbsp	all-purpose flour	25 mL
1 tbsp	tomato paste	15 mL
2 cups	dark beer	500 mL
½ cup	chicken stock (store-bought or see recipe, page 135)	125 mL
2	bay leaves	2
1 tbsp	paprika (see tips), dissolved in 2 tbsp (25 mL) cider vinegar	15 mL
8 cups	thinly sliced (chiffonade) stemmed collard greens (about 2 bunches) (see tips)	2 L

MAKE AHEAD

Complete Step 3, heating 1 tbsp (15 mL) oil in pan before softening the onions. Cover and refrigerate for up to 2 days. When you're ready to cook, sauté the bacon and brown the beef. Combine meat and vegetable mixture and continue with Step 4.

• Works in slow cookers from 3½ to 6 quarts

1. In a large skillet, cook bacon over medium–high heat until crisp. Remove with a slotted spoon and drain on a paper towel. Cover and refrigerate until ready to use. Drain off all but 1 tbsp (15 mL) fat from pan, reserving remainder.

2. Add beef to pan, in batches, and cook, stirring, until lightly browned, about 4 minutes per batch, adding more bacon drippings between batches if necessary. Using a slotted spoon, transfer to slow cooker stoneware as completed.

3. Reduce heat to medium. Add onions to pan, adding more bacon drippings if necessary, and cook, stirring, until softened, about 3 minutes. Add garlic, thyme, salt and peppercorns; cook, stirring, for 1 minute. Add flour and cook, stirring, until lightly browned, about 2 minutes. Stir in tomato paste. Add beer, stock and bay leaves; bring to a boil. Cook, stirring, for 1 minute, scraping up any brown bits in the pan. Transfer to stoneware and stir well.

4. Cover and cook on Low for 8 hours or on High for 4 hours, until beef is tender. Stir in paprika solution and reserved bacon. Add collard greens, in batches, completely submerging each batch in liquid before adding another. Cover and cook on High for 30 minutes, until collards are tender. Discard bay leaves.

TIPS

I prefer to use sweet paprika in this recipe, but if you like a bit of heat, use hot paprika instead, reducing the quantity to 2 tsp (10 mL). Smoked paprika would also work, adding a pleasant bit of smokiness to the dish.

One way to prepare collard greens for use in a stew is to cut them into a chiffonade. Remove any tough veins toward the bottom of the leaves and up the center of the lower portion of the leaf. Stack about 6 in a pile. Roll them up like a cigar, then slice as thinly as you can. Repeat until all the greens are sliced.

Greek-Style Beef with Eggplant

This ambrosial stew reminds me of moussaka without the topping, and it is far less work. Made with red wine and lycopene-rich tomato paste, it develops a deep and intriguing flavor. Serve with steamed broccoli and a tossed green salad for a delicious and nutrient-rich meal. **Serves 6**

2	eggplants (each about 1 lb/500 g) peeled, halved and each half cut into quarters	2
2 tbsp	kosher salt	25 mL
2 tbsp	olive oil, divided	25 mL
1 lb	lean ground beef	500 g
4	onions, thinly sliced on the vertical	4
4	cloves garlic, minced	4
2 tsp	dried oregano, crumbled	10 mL
1 tsp	ground cinnamon	5 mL
½ tsp	salt	2 mL
½ tsp	cracked black peppercorns	2 mL
1	can (5½ oz/156 mL) tomato paste	1
1 cup	dry red wine	250 mL
1 cup	packed fresh parsley leaves, finely chopped	250 mL
	Hot cooked bulgur (see tip)	
	Freshly grated Parmesan cheese	

MAKE AHEAD

Complete Steps 1 to 3, placing eggplant and meat mixtures in separate containers. Cover and refrigerate for up to 2 days. When you're ready to cook, combine mixtures in stoneware and continue with the recipe.

- Works in slow cookers from 3½ to 6 quarts
- Large rimmed baking sheet

1. Place eggplant in a colander over a sink and sprinkle with kosher salt. Toss to ensure eggplant is well coated and set aside for 30 to 60 minutes. Meanwhile, preheat oven to 400°F (200°C).

2. Rinse eggplant well under cold running water and drain. Pat dry with a paper towel. Brush all over with 1 tbsp (15 mL) of the oil. Place on baking sheet and bake until soft and fragrant, about 20 minutes. Transfer to slow cooker stoneware.

3. Meanwhile, in a skillet, heat the remaining oil over medium heat for 30 seconds. Add ground beef and onions; cook, stirring and breaking meat up with a spoon, until beef is no longer pink, about 10 minutes. Add garlic, oregano, cinnamon, salt and peppercorns; cook, stirring, for 1 minute. Stir in tomato paste and wine. Transfer to stoneware and stir well.

4. Cover and cook on Low for 8 hours or on High for 4 hours, until mixture is bubbly and eggplant is tender. Stir in parsley.

5. Ladle over hot bulgur and pass the Parmesan at the table.

> **TIP**
>
> To cook bulgur to accompany this recipe, combine 2 cups (500 mL) medium or fine bulgur and 4 cups (1 L) boiling water. Cover and set aside until water is absorbed and bulgur is tender to the bite, about 20 minutes.

Savory Lamb Shanks with Eggplant and Barley

Here's a rich, delicious Mediterranean-inspired stew that will warm the cockles of your heart on a chilly night. Lamb shanks are succulent, and the dish is loaded with flavor.

Serves 6 to 8

1	large eggplant (about 1½ lbs/750 g), peeled and cut into 2-inch (5 cm) cubes	1
	Salt	
4 lbs	sliced lamb shanks (see tips), patted dry	2 kg
½ tsp	salt	2 mL
½ tsp	cracked black peppercorns	2 mL
2 tbsp	olive oil (approx.), divided	25 mL
2	onions, thinly sliced on the vertical	2
4	cloves garlic, minced	4
2	bay leaves	2
1	stick cinnamon, about 2 inches (5 cm) long	1
1 tbsp	finely grated lemon zest	15 mL
1 cup	barley (see tips), rinsed and drained	250 mL
1 cup	dry red wine	250 mL
1	can (28 oz/796 mL) diced tomatoes, with juice	1
¼ cup	finely chopped fresh parsley	50 mL

MAKE AHEAD

Complete Steps 1 and 3, adding oil to the pan to sauté eggplant. Cover and refrigerate for up to 2 days. When you're ready to cook, brown the lamb shanks and continue with the recipe.

- **Works best in a large (minimum 5-quart) slow cooker**

1. Place eggplant in a colander over a sink and sprinkle with salt. Toss well and set aside for 1 to 2 hours. (If time is short, blanch eggplant cubes in heavily salted water.) Rinse well under cold running water and, using your hands, squeeze out excess moisture. Pat dry with a paper towel and set aside.

2. Season lamb shanks with salt and peppercorns. In a skillet, heat 1 tbsp (15 mL) of the oil over medium-high heat for 30 seconds. Add lamb, in batches, and brown well on all sides, about 4 minutes per batch. Transfer to slow cooker stoneware as completed. Drain off all but 2 tbsp (15 mL) fat, if necessary. (If your lamb is very lean, you may need to add a bit of oil here.)

3. Add eggplant to pan, in batches, and cook, stirring, until lightly browned, adding more oil if necessary. Transfer to slow cooker stoneware as completed.

4. Add onions to pan and cook, stirring, until lightly browned, about 7 minutes. Add garlic, bay leaves, cinnamon stick and lemon zest; cook, stirring, for 1 minute. Add barley and toss to coat. Add wine and tomatoes with juice; bring to a boil. Transfer to slow cooker stoneware.

5. Cover and cook on Low for 10 to 12 hours or on High for 5 to 6 hours, until the meat is falling off the bone. Discard bay leaves and cinnamon stick.

TIPS

Have your butcher slice the shanks for you. Depending on their size, you'll get from 2 to 4 pieces from each shank.

Use the kind of barley you prefer — pearled, pot and whole all work well in this recipe.

To give this recipe a Moroccan spin, substitute a finely chopped preserved lemon for the lemon zest. Add it along with the tomatoes.

Chunky Black Bean Chili

Here's a great-tasting, stick-to-your-ribs chili that is perfect for a family dinner or a casual evening with friends. Serve this with crusty bread, a green salad and robust red wine or cold beer. **Serves 8**

1 tbsp	vegetable oil (approx.)	15 mL
2 lbs	stewing beef, trimmed, cut into 1-inch (2.5 cm) cubes and patted dry	1 kg
2	onions, finely chopped	2
4	cloves garlic, minced	4
1 tbsp	cumin seeds, toasted and ground (see tip, page 64)	15 mL
1 tbsp	dried oregano, crumbled	15 mL
1 tsp	cracked black peppercorns	5 mL
1 tsp	salt	5 mL
1	can (28 oz/796 mL) diced tomatoes, with juice	1
1½ cups	flat beer or beef stock, divided	375 mL
4 cups	cooked black beans, drained and rinsed	1 L
2	dried ancho chiles	2
2	dried New Mexico chiles	2
4 cups	boiling water	1 L
1 cup	coarsely chopped fresh cilantro	250 mL
1 to 2	jalapeño peppers, chopped (optional)	1 to 2

MAKE AHEAD

Complete Step 2, heating 1 tbsp (15 mL) oil in pan before softening the onions. Cover and refrigerate for up to 2 days. When you're ready to cook, brown the beef, or if you're pressed for time, omit this step. Continue with the recipe.

• **Works best in a large (minimum 5-quart) slow cooker**

1. In a skillet, heat oil over medium–high heat for 30 seconds. Add beef, in batches, and cook, stirring, until lightly browned, about 4 minutes per batch, adding a bit more oil between batches if necessary. Transfer to slow cooker stoneware as completed.

2. Reduce heat to medium. Add onions and cook, stirring, until softened, about 3 minutes. Add garlic, cumin, oregano, peppercorns and salt; cook, stirring, for 1 minute. Add tomatoes with juice and cook, breaking up with the back of a spoon. Add 1 cup (250 mL) of the beer and bring to a boil. Transfer to stoneware and stir well.

3. Stir in beans. Cover and cook on Low for 8 to 10 hours or on High for 4 to 5 hours, until beef is tender.

4. About an hour before recipe has finished cooking, combine ancho chiles, New Mexico chiles and boiling water in a heatproof bowl. Set aside for 30 minutes, weighing down chiles with a cup to ensure they remain submerged. Drain, discarding soaking liquid and stems, and coarsely chop chiles. Transfer to a blender and add cilantro, jalapeños (if using) and the remaining beer; purée.

5. Add chile mixture to stoneware and stir well. Cover and cook on High for 30 minutes until mixture is hot and bubbly and flavors meld.

6. Ladle into bowls and garnish as desired (see tips).

TIPS

If you prefer, you can use 2 cups (250 mL) dried black beans, soaked, cooked and drained (see Basic Beans, page 133), instead of the canned beans.

Garnish this chili with any combination of sour cream, finely chopped red or green onion, shredded Monterey Jack cheese and/or salsa.

Butternut Chili

I love this chili. The combination of beef, butternut squash, ancho chiles and cilantro is a real winner. Don't be afraid to make extra — it's great reheated.

Serves 6

1 tbsp	vegetable oil	15 mL
1 lb	lean ground beef	500 g
2	onions, finely chopped	2
4	cloves garlic, minced	4
1	stick cinnamon, about 2 inches (5 cm) long	1
1 tbsp	cumin seeds, toasted and ground (see tip, page 64)	15 mL
2 tsp	dried oregano	10 mL
1 tsp	salt	5 mL
½ tsp	cracked black peppercorns	2 mL
1	can (28 oz/796 mL) diced tomatoes, with juice	1
3 cups	cubed butternut squash (1-inch/2.5 cm cubes)	750 mL
2 cups	canned kidney beans, drained and rinsed	500 mL
2	dried New Mexico, ancho or guajillo chiles	2
2 cups	boiling water	500 mL
½ cup	coarsely chopped fresh cilantro	125 mL

MAKE AHEAD

Complete Steps 1 and 3. Cover and refrigerate tomato and chile mixtures separately overnight. The next morning, continue with the recipe.

- Works best in a large (minimum 5-quart) slow cooker

1. In a skillet, heat oil over medium–high heat for 30 seconds. Add beef and onions; cook, stirring and breaking meat up with a spoon, until beef is no longer pink, about 10 minutes. Add garlic, cinnamon stick, cumin, oregano, salt and peppercorns; cook, stirring, for 1 minute. Add tomatoes with juice and bring to a boil.

2. Place squash and beans in slow cooker stoneware and cover with beef mixture. Cover and cook on Low for 6 to 8 hours or on High for 3 to 4 hours, until squash is tender.

3. About an hour before recipe has finished cooking, combine dried chiles and boiling water in a heatproof bowl. Set aside for 30 minutes, weighing down chiles with a cup to ensure they remain submerged. Drain, reserving ½ cup (125 mL) of the soaking liquid. Discard stems and coarsely chop chiles. Transfer to a blender and add cilantro and reserved soaking liquid; purée.

4. Add chile mixture to stoneware and stir well. Cover and cook on High for 30 minutes, until mixture is hot and bubbly and flavors meld. Discard cinnamon stick.

TIPS

You can use 1 cup (250 mL) dried kidney beans, soaked, cooked and drained (see Basic Beans, page 133), instead of the canned beans.

If you prefer, you can soak and purée the chiles while preparing the chili and refrigerate until you're ready to add them to the recipe.

Sunday Pot Roast with Cumin-Spiked Barley

Here's a Sunday dinner dish that's reminiscent of old-fashioned country kitchens. Just add some sliced green beans and, perhaps, hot whole-grain rolls to soak up the gravy. **Serves 8**

¼ cup	all-purpose flour	50 mL
1 tsp	dried thyme	5 mL
½ tsp	salt (or to taste)	2 mL
½ tsp	cracked black pepper	2 mL
3 lbs	boneless beef pot roast	1.5 kg
1 tbsp	olive oil (approx.)	15 mL
2	onions, finely chopped	2
3	carrots, peeled and diced	3
4	stalks celery, diced	4
4	cloves garlic, minced	4
1	bay leaf	1
2 tbsp	ground cumin	25 mL
1 cup	barley (see tips) rinsed and drained	250 mL
2 cups	water	500 mL
2 cups	beef stock	500 mL
1 cup	dry red wine	250 mL
½ cup	chopped parsley	125 mL

VARIATION

Sunday Pot Roast with Cumin-Spiked Wheat Berries
Substitute wheat, spelt or Kamut berries for the barley.

MAKE AHEAD

Complete Step 3, heating 1 tbsp (15 mL) oil in pan before softening the vegetables. Cover and refrigerate for up to 2 days. When you're ready to cook, continue with the recipe, cooking on High for at least the first 2 hours to compensate for the cold vegetable mixture.

- Works best in a large (minimum 5-quart) slow cooker

1. On a plate, combine flour, thyme, salt and pepper. Dredge roast, covering all sides, and set any remaining flour mixture aside.

2. In a skillet, heat oil over medium heat for 30 seconds. Add roast and brown on all sides, about 8 minutes. Transfer to slow cooker stoneware.

3. Add more oil to pan, if necessary. Add onions, carrots and celery; cook, stirring, until softened, about 7 minutes. Add garlic, bay leaf and cumin; cook, stirring, for 1 minute. Add reserved flour mixture and cook, stirring, for 1 minute. Add barley and toss to coat. Add water, stock and wine; bring to a boil. Pour over roast, making sure it thoroughly coats the meat.

4. Cover and cook on Low for 10 hours or on High for 5 hours, until meat is very tender. Discard bay leaf. Taste and add salt and pepper, if necessary.

5. Transfer meat to a deep platter or serving dish and slice thinly. Cover with sauce and garnish with parsley.

TIPS

For the best flavor, toast and grind whole cumin seeds rather than buying ground cumin. Simply stir seeds in a dry skillet over medium heat until fragrant, about 3 minutes. Immediately transfer to a spice grinder or mortar and grind.

Use the variety of barley you prefer — pearled, pot or whole. Whole (also known as hulled) barley is the most nutritious form of the grain.

Fragrant Beef Curry with Barley

Make this delicious curry any time you have a craving for something lusciously different. It's a great Sunday night dinner and is perfect for a potluck or on a buffet.

Serves 6 to 8

2 tbsp	olive oil (approx.), divided	25 mL
2 lbs	stewing beef, trimmed, cut into 1-inch (2.5 cm) cubes and patted dry	1 kg
2	onions, finely chopped	2
4	cloves garlic, minced	4
4	whole cloves	4
3	black cardamom pods, crushed	3
2	bay leaves	2
1	stick cinnamon, about 3 inches (7.5 cm) long	1
1 tbsp	minced gingerroot	15 mL
1 tsp	ground turmeric	5 mL
1 tsp	salt	5 mL
1 tsp	cracked black peppercorns	5 mL
1 cup	barley, rinsed and drained	250 mL
2 cups	chicken stock (store-bought or see recipe, page 135)	500 mL
1 to 2	long red or green chile peppers, seeded and diced	1 to 2
1 cup	full-fat plain yogurt	250 mL
1 tsp	sweet paprika	5 mL
¼ tsp	cayenne pepper	1 mL
¼ cup	finely chopped fresh cilantro	50 mL

VARIATION

Spicy Lamb Curry with Barley
Substitute stewing lamb for the beef.

MAKE AHEAD

See page 72.

- **Works best in a large (minimum 5-quart) slow cooker**

1. In a skillet, heat 1 tbsp (15 mL) of the oil over medium heat for 30 seconds. Add beef, in batches, and cook, stirring, until lightly browned, about 4 minutes per batch, adding a bit more oil between batches if necessary. Using a slotted spoon, transfer to slow cooker stoneware as completed. Reduce heat to medium and add the remaining oil to pan.

2. Add onions and cook, stirring, until softened, about 3 minutes. Add garlic, cloves, cardamom, bay leaves, cinnamon stick, ginger, turmeric, salt and peppercorns; cook, stirring, for 1 minute. Add barley and toss to coat. Stir in stock and bring to a boil. Transfer to stoneware and stir well.

3. Cover and cook on Low for 8 hours or on High for 4 hours, until beef and barley are tender. Discard cloves, cardamom, bay leaves and cinnamon stick.

4. In a small bowl, combine chiles, yogurt, paprika and cayenne. Stir into beef mixture. Cover and cook on Low for 15 minutes, until flavors meld. When serving, garnish with cilantro and accompany with your favorite chutney and warm naan, if desired.

TIP

Use pearled, pot or whole barley in this recipe — whichever you prefer. Whole (also known as hulled) barley is the most nutritious form of the grain.

The Best Beef Daube

With its robust Provençal flavors, daube is French comfort food, and this one is particularly tasty. Although it takes a long time to make, it is really a series of small steps completed over the course of 3 days. I love the addition of short ribs, which contribute fabulous flavor to the dish, but they also add fat. As a result, it makes sense to let the cooked daube sit overnight in the refrigerator. When you're ready to serve, the fat can be easily skimmed off before the dish is reheated in the oven. Hot orzo, tossed with freshly grated Parmesan cheese and some of the cooking juices, makes a superb accompaniment, but daube is also delicious over noodles or mashed potatoes.

Serves 8

3 lbs	beef chuck, cut into thin slices (about ¼ inch/0.5 cm) and patted dry	1.5 kg
2½ to 3 lbs	beef short ribs	1.25 to 1.5 kg
4	cloves garlic, minced	4
2	onions, thinly sliced	2
2	carrots, peeled and diced	2
4	whole cloves	4
3	sprigs fresh thyme (or ½ tsp/2 mL dried thyme)	3
2	bay leaves	2
½ tsp	cracked black peppercorns	2 mL
1	bottle (750 mL) robust red wine	1
4	slices bacon	4
	Coarse sea salt	
2 tbsp	tomato paste	25 mL

VARIATION

Garnished Daube

In a small bowl, combine ½ cup (125 mL) pitted finely chopped black olives and ¼ cup (50 mL) finely chopped fresh parsley leaves. Pass at the table.

MAKE AHEAD

This dish should be completed at least 1 day ahead to maximize the flavor.

- **Works best in a large (minimum 5-quart) slow cooker**

1. In a large bowl, combine beef chuck, short ribs, garlic, onions, carrots, cloves, thyme, bay leaves, peppercorns and wine. Cover and refrigerate overnight or for up to 2 days. Drain, reserving vegetables, meat and liquid separately.

2. In a skillet, cook bacon over medium-high heat until crisp. Drain on paper towel and crumble. Set aside. Drain off all but 2 tbsp (25 mL) fat from pan.

3. Reduce heat to medium. Add reserved vegetables to pan and cook, stirring, until softened, about 7 minutes. Transfer to slow cooker stoneware.

4. Increase heat to medium-high. Add reserved meat, in batches, and brown on both sides, about 5 minutes per batch. Using a slotted spoon, transfer to stoneware as completed, sprinkling each layer with bacon and sea salt.

5. Add tomato paste and reserved liquid to pan and heat just to the boiling point, scraping up any brown bits stuck to pan. Add to stoneware.

6. Cover and cook on Low for 8 to 10 hours or on High for 4 to 5 hours, until ribs are falling off the bone. Transfer to a large bowl. Let cool, cover and refrigerate overnight.

7. Forty-five minutes before you're ready to serve, preheat oven to 350°F (180°C). Skim fat off daube and discard. Transfer meat, with sauce, to a large oven-to-table serving dish, cover loosely with foil and heat for 30 minutes.

Savory Short Ribs

These robust short ribs are delicious and make a great casual dinner with friends. I like to serve them with hot orzo tossed with extra-virgin olive oil and sprinkled with Parmesan. Add a tossed green salad, crusty rolls and some robust red wine to finish the meal.　　**Serves 6**

1 tbsp	cracked black peppercorns	15 mL
1 tbsp	dried thyme	15 mL
1 tbsp	fennel seeds, toasted and ground (see tips)	15 mL
2 tbsp	extra-virgin olive oil	25 mL
4 lbs	beef short ribs	2 kg
4 oz	bacon, finely chopped	125 g
2	each onions and carrots, peeled and finely chopped	2
4	cloves garlic, minced	4
4	anchovy fillets, minced	4
1 tsp	salt	5 mL
½ tsp	cracked black peppercorns	2 mL
1 cup	robust red wine	250 mL
1 tbsp	red wine vinegar	15 mL
1	can (28 oz/796 mL) diced tomatoes, with juice	1
1	bouquet garni (see tips)	1
1 cup	chopped pitted black olives	250 mL

- Works best in a large (minimum 5-quart) slow cooker

1. In a baking dish large enough to accommodate the short ribs, combine the 1 tbsp (15 mL) peppercorns, thyme, fennel and oil. Add ribs, turning until evenly coated. Cover and refrigerate overnight.

2. Preheat broiler and position broiler rack 6 inches (15 cm) from the heat source. Broil ribs, turning once, until well browned on both sides, about 10 minutes per side. Drain on paper towels. Separate ribs, if in strips, and place in slow cooker stoneware.

3. In a skillet, cook bacon over medium–high heat, stirring, until crisp. Using a slotted spoon, transfer to stoneware. Drain off all but 1 tbsp (15 mL) fat from pan.

4. Reduce heat to medium. Add onions and carrots to pan and cook, stirring, until carrots are softened, about 7 minutes. Add garlic, anchovies, salt and the ½ tsp (2 mL) peppercorns; cook, stirring, for 1 minute. Add wine and vinegar; cook, stirring, for 2 minutes. Stir in tomatoes with juice and bouquet garni. Transfer to stoneware.

5. Cover and cook on Low for 10 to 12 hours or on High for 5 to 6 hours, until ribs are falling off the bone. Discard bouquet garni. Stir in olives.

MAKE AHEAD

Marinate ribs and complete Step 4. Cover and refrigerate overnight. Then complete the recipe, but don't add the olives. Cover and refrigerate for up to 2 days. When you're ready to serve, preheat oven to 350°F (180°C). Skim fat off ribs and discard. Transfer to a large oven-to-table serving dish. Cover loosely with foil and heat for 20 minutes. Stir in olives. Continue heating until sauce is hot and bubbly, about 10 minutes.

TIPS

Toasting fennel seeds intensifies their flavor. To toast fennel seeds, stir them in a dry skillet over medium heat until fragrant, about 3 minutes. Transfer to a mortar or spice grinder and grind.

To make a bouquet garni, tie your favorite herbs (such as parsley, thyme and bay leaf) together or place them in a cheesecloth bag.

Citrus Lamb with Spinach and Couscous

In the Middle East, sun-dried limes often add pleasant pungency to dishes. Here, I've tried to capture some of their unique character. Prominent citrus flavors balance the richness of the saffron and lamb, and slightly bitter spinach adds to the pleasing complexity. Couscous makes the perfect finish.

Serves 6

2 tbsp	olive oil (approx.)	25 mL
1½ lbs	trimmed lamb shoulder, cut into 1-inch (2.5 cm) cubes	750 g
2	onions, thinly sliced on the vertical	2
4	cloves garlic, minced	4
1 tbsp	finely grated lime zest	15 mL
1 tsp	cracked black peppercorns	5 mL
½ tsp	salt	2 mL
3½ cups	chicken stock (store-bought or see recipe, page 135), divided	875 mL
¼ cup	freshly squeezed lime juice	50 mL
½ tsp	crumbled saffron threads, dissolved in ¼ cup (50 mL) boiling water	2 mL
1 lb	spinach, stems removed and leaves finely chopped (see tips)	500 g
1 cup	couscous, preferably whole-grain (see tips)	250 mL

MAKE AHEAD

Complete Step 2, heating 1 tbsp (15 mL) of the oil in pan before softening the onions. Cover and refrigerate for up to 2 days. When you're ready to cook, brown the meat and continue with the recipe.

- **Works best in a large (minimum 5-quart) slow cooker**

1. In a skillet, heat 1 tbsp (15 mL) of the oil over medium–high heat for 30 seconds. Add lamb, in batches, and cook, stirring, until lightly browned, about 4 minutes per batch, adding a bit more oil between batches if necessary. Using a slotted spoon, transfer to slow cooker stoneware as completed.

2. Reduce heat to medium. Add onions to pan and cook, stirring, until they begin to brown, about 7 minutes. Add garlic, lime zest, peppercorns and salt; cook, stirring, for 30 seconds. Add 2 cups (500 mL) of the stock, lime juice and saffron mixture; bring to a boil. Transfer to stoneware and stir well.

3. Cover and cook on Low for 8 hours or on High for 4 hours, until lamb is tender. Stir in spinach. Cover and cook on High until spinach is wilted, about 15 minutes.

4. Meanwhile, in a saucepan, bring the remaining stock to a boil over medium heat. Add couscous in a steady stream, stirring constantly. Remove from heat. Cover and let stand until liquid is absorbed, about 15 minutes. Fluff with a fork.

5. Spread couscous over a deep platter. Arrange lamb mixture evenly over top, leaving a border around the edges.

TIPS

Spinach that hasn't been prewashed can be quite gritty, so pay extra attention when washing. I always swish the leaves around in a basin of lukewarm water to remove any grit, then rinse thoroughly under cold running water before using.

Use whole wheat, spelt, Kamut or barley couscous in this recipe. It is much more nutritious than couscous made from refined flour and is just as easy to prepare.

Pork Pozole

I love the robust flavors in this traditional Mexican dish, perfect for a casual evening with friends. Add the chipotle if you like heat and a bit of smoke. To continue the Mexican theme, serve with warm tortillas and a tossed green salad that includes a diced avocado. **Serves 6**

4	slices bacon	4
2 lbs	boneless pork shoulder blade (butt), trimmed and cut into 1-inch (2.5 cm) cubes	1 kg
2	onions, finely chopped	2
4	cloves garlic, minced	4
1 tbsp	dried oregano	15 mL
2 tsp	finely grated lime zest	10 mL
½ tsp	cracked black pepper	2 mL
2 cups	canned diced tomatoes, with juice	500 mL
1	can (29 oz/824 mL) hominy, drained	1
1½ cups	chicken stock	375 mL
2	dried ancho or guajillo chiles	2
2 cups	boiling water	500 mL
1	chipotle pepper in adobo sauce (optional)	1
2 tbsp	finely chopped fresh cilantro	25 mL
2 tbsp	freshly squeezed lime juice	25 mL
2	poblano or green bell peppers, diced	2
	Salt	

MAKE AHEAD

Complete Steps 1, 3 and 5. Cover and refrigerate bacon, vegetable mixture and chile mixture separately for up to 2 days. (The chile mixture will lose some of its vibrancy. For best results, complete Step 3 while the chili is cooking.) When you're ready to cook, brown the pork and continue with the recipe.

- Works best in a large (minimum 5-quart) slow cooker

1. In a skillet, cook bacon over medium-high heat until crisp. Drain on a paper towel and crumble. Cover and refrigerate until ready to use. Drain off all but 2 tbsp (25 mL) fat from pan, reserving remainder.

2. Add pork to pan, in batches, and cook, stirring, until lightly browned, about 3 minutes per batch, adding more bacon drippings between batches if necessary. Using a slotted spoon, transfer to a plate as completed.

3. Reduce heat to medium. Add onions to pan and cook, stirring, until softened, about 3 minutes. Add garlic, oregano, lime zest and pepper; cook, stirring, for 1 minute. Add reserved pork and any accumulated juices, tomatoes with juice, hominy and stock; bring to a boil. Transfer to slow cooker stoneware.

4. Cover and cook on Low for 8 hours or on High for 4 hours, until pork is tender.

5. About an hour before recipe has finished cooking, combine dried chiles and boiling water in a heatproof bowl. Set aside for 30 minutes, weighing chiles down with a cup to ensure they remain submerged. Drain, discarding soaking liquid and stems, and coarsely chop chiles. Transfer to a blender and add chipotle pepper (if using), cilantro, lime juice and ½ cup (125 mL) broth from the pork mixture; purée.

6. Add chile mixture to stoneware, along with reserved bacon and poblano peppers, and stir well. Stir in salt to taste. Cover and cook on High for 30 minutes, until peppers are tender and flavors meld.

7. Ladle into soup plates and garnish as desired (see tip).

> **TIP**
> Garnish with shredded lettuce, chopped radish, chopped red or green onion and fried tortilla strips, as desired. Pass lime wedges for diners to squeeze over their pork.

Mediterranean Pork and Beans

This dish is loaded with flavor. To complement the Mediterranean ingredients, I like to accompany this with a platter of marinated roasted peppers. Add warm crusty bread, such as ciabatta — and, if you're feeling festive, a robust Rioja. It makes a large quantity but reheats well. **Serves 8**

1 tbsp	puréed garlic (see tips)	15 mL
1 tsp	salt	5 mL
½ tsp	cracked black pepper	2 mL
2 lbs	boneless pork shoulder blade (butt), trimmed and cut into bite-size pieces	1 kg
2 tbsp	olive oil (approx.), divided	25 mL
6	anchovy fillets, minced	6
3	onions, thinly sliced	3
2 tsp	dried thyme	10 mL
1 cup	dry white wine	250 mL
1 tsp	white wine vinegar	5 mL
1	can (14 oz/398 mL) diced tomatoes, with juice	1
4 cups	canned white beans, drained and rinsed	1 L
1 cup	finely chopped fresh parsley	250 mL
1 cup	chopped pitted kalamata olives (about 48)	250 mL
1 tsp	paprika (preferably smoked), dissolved in 1 tbsp (15 mL) white wine or water	5 mL

MAKE AHEAD

Complete Step 1. Heat 1 tbsp (15 mL) of the oil and complete Step 3. Cover and refrigerate meat and onion mixtures separately for up to 2 days. When you're ready to cook, continue with the recipe.

- **Works best in a large (minimum 5-quart) slow cooker**

1. In a bowl large enough to accommodate the pork, combine garlic, salt and pepper. Add pork and toss to coat. Cover and refrigerate overnight.

2. In a skillet, heat 1 tbsp (15 mL) of the oil over medium–high heat for 30 seconds. Pat pork dry with paper towels and add to pan, in batches; cook, stirring, until lightly browned, about 5 minutes per batch, adding a bit more oil between batches if necessary. Using a slotted spoon, transfer to slow cooker stoneware as completed.

3. Reduce heat to medium and add more oil to the pan if necessary. Add anchovies and onions; cook, stirring, until onions are softened, about 3 minutes. Add thyme and cook, stirring, for 1 minute. Add wine and vinegar; cook for 2 minutes, stirring and scraping up any brown bits on the bottom of the pan. Add tomatoes with juice and bring to a boil. Transfer to stoneware and stir well.

4. Stir in beans. Cover and cook on Low for 8 to 10 hours or on High for 4 to 5 hours, until pork is very tender (it should be falling apart). Stir in parsley, olives and paprika solution. Cover and cook on High for 15 minutes, until heated through.

TIPS

To purée garlic, use a fine, sharp-toothed grater, such as those made by Microplane.

If you prefer, you can use 2 cups (250 mL) dried white kidney or navy beans, soaked, cooked and drained (see Basic Beans, page 133), instead of the canned beans.

Baked Beans 'n' Barley

If you're a fan of Boston baked beans, this dish is for you. It's every bit as delicious as the best versions of the original. This is the perfect choice for a chilly day or a potluck or tailgate party. If you're serving it for dinner, complete the meal with warm whole-grain rolls and a tossed green salad.

Serves 6

¾ cup	ketchup	175 mL
⅔ cup	pure maple syrup (see tips)	150 mL
4	cloves garlic, minced	4
1 tbsp	minced gingerroot	15 mL
1 tsp	dry mustard	5 mL
1 tsp	salt	5 mL
1 tsp	cracked black peppercorns	5 mL
4 oz	chunk pancetta or salt pork, diced	125 g
2	onions, halved and thinly sliced on the vertical	2
1 cup	barley (see tips), rinsed and drained	250 mL
1 cup	dried navy beans, soaked, cooked and drained (see Basic Beans, page 133), cooking liquid reserved	250 mL
2	dried red chile peppers (optional)	2

VARIATION

Baked Beans 'n' Wheat Berries
Substitute an equal quantity of wheat, spelt or Kamut berries for the barley.

Crusty Baked Beans 'n' Barley
Forty-five minutes before you're ready to serve, preheat oven to 325°F (160°C). Stir in chile peppers, if using, as per Step 2, but do not cook to meld flavors. If your stoneware insert isn't ovenproof, transfer mixture to a baking dish or individual ramekins. Bake until top is crusty, about 30 minutes. Remove and discard chile peppers, if using.

- **Works best in a large (minimum 5-quart) slow cooker**

1. In a bowl, combine ketchup, maple syrup, garlic, ginger, dry mustard, salt and peppercorns. Set aside.

2. In slow cooker stoneware, combine pancetta, onions, barley, beans and ketchup mixture. Stir well. Add reserved bean liquid barely to cover. Cover and cook on Low for 8 hours or on High for 4 hours. Stir in chile peppers, if using. Cover and cook on High for 30 minutes to meld flavors.

TIPS
Although any kind of maple syrup works well in this recipe, I like to use the dark amber or grade B versions, which are more strongly flavored. They are also more economical than the lighter kinds.

Use pearled, pot or whole barley in this recipe — whichever you prefer. Whole (also known as hulled) barley is the most nutritious form of the grain.

If you like heat, the chile peppers add a pleasant note, but they are not essential.

Ribs in Tablecloth Stainer Sauce

The colorful name of this Mexican sauce, which is distinguished by the addition of fruit, is a literal translation from the Spanish. You can vary the quantity of chiles to suit your taste; three produce a pleasantly spicy sauce. Serve this with warm tortillas to soak up the ambrosial liquid.

Serves 6

4 lbs	country-style pork ribs (see tip)	2 kg
1 tbsp	vegetable oil	15 mL
2	onions, thinly sliced on the vertical	2
4	cloves garlic, minced	4
1	stick cinnamon, about 2 inches (5 cm) long	1
1 tbsp	dried oregano	15 mL
1 tsp	salt	5 mL
½ tsp	cracked black pepper	2 mL
6	whole allspice	6
2	apples, peeled, cored and sliced	2
1	can (14 oz/398 mL) diced tomatoes, with juice	1
1 cup	chicken stock (store-bought or see recipe, page 135), divided	250 mL
3	dried ancho chiles	3
3 cups	boiling water	750 mL
2	bananas, sliced	2
1	jalapeño pepper, seeded and coarsely chopped	1
1 tbsp	cider vinegar	15 mL
1 cup	pineapple chunks, drained if canned	250 mL

MAKE AHEAD

Complete Step 2. Cover and refrigerate for up to 2 days. When you're ready to cook, broil the ribs and continue with the recipe.

- Preheat broiler, with rack 6 inches (15 cm) from heat source
- Works best in a large (minimum 5-quart) slow cooker

1. Broil ribs, turning once, until lightly browned on both sides, about 7 minutes per side. Drain on paper towels and transfer to slow cooker stoneware.

2. In a skillet, heat oil over medium heat for 30 seconds. Add onions and cook, stirring, until softened, about 3 minutes. Add garlic, cinnamon stick, oregano, salt, peppercorns and allspice; cook, stirring, for 1 minute. Add apples, tomatoes with juice and ½ cup (125 mL) of the stock; bring to a boil.

3. Pour sauce over ribs. Cover and cook on Low for 5 hours or on High for 2½ hours, until ribs are tender and falling off the bone.

4. About an hour before recipe has finished cooking, combine ancho chiles and boiling water in a heatproof bowl. Set aside for 30 minutes, weighing chiles down with a cup to ensure they remain submerged. Drain, discarding soaking liquid and stems, and coarsely chop chiles. Transfer to a blender and add bananas, jalapeño, vinegar and the remaining stock; purée.

5. Add chile mixture to stoneware, along with pineapple, and stir well. Cover and cook on High for 30 minutes, until hot and bubbly and flavors meld. Discard cinnamon stick and allspice.

TIP

This recipe works best if the ribs are in one big piece when cooked. (In my experience, this cut is usually available only from a butcher or in the pork roast section of the grocery store.) The single piece is easy to turn while broiling and will basically fall apart into individual servings after the meat is cooked.

Sausage-Spiked Peas 'n' Rice

What could be easier than this combination of brown and wild rice and split peas, seasoned with sausage and fennel? The flavors are fantastic, and I love the way the split peas dissolve into the sauce, creating a luscious texture I find extremely satisfying. Add a simple green salad or some steamed green beans and enjoy.   **Serves 6**

1 tbsp	olive oil	15 mL
12 oz	hot or mild Italian sausage, removed from casings	375 g
1	bulb fennel, cored and chopped	1
1	onion, finely chopped	1
4	cloves garlic, minced	4
1 cup	brown and wild rice mixture (see tips), rinsed and drained	250 mL
1 tsp	dried thyme (see tips)	5 mL
½ tsp	cracked black peppercorns	2 mL
2 cups	chicken stock (store-bought or see recipe, page 135)	500 mL
2 cups	cooked yellow split peas, with ¼ cup (50 mL) cooking liquid (see tips)	500 mL

MAKE AHEAD

Complete Step 1. Cover and refrigerate for up to 2 days. When you're ready to cook, continue with the recipe.

- Works best in a large (minimum 5-quart) slow cooker.

1. In a large skillet, heat oil over medium heat for 30 seconds. Add sausage, fennel and onion; cook, stirring and breaking meat up with a spoon, until sausage is no longer pink, about 6 minutes. Add garlic, rice, thyme and peppercorns; cook, stirring, for 1 minute. Stir in stock and peas with reserved liquid; bring to a boil. Transfer to slow cooker stoneware.

2. Place a clean tea towel, folded in half (so you will have two layers), over top of stoneware, to absorb the moisture. (Accumulated moisture affects the consistency of the rice. The tea towel will absorb the moisture generated during cooking.) Cover and cook on Low for 8 hours or on High for 4 hours, until wild rice is tender and grains begin to split.

TIPS

There are many very nice packaged rice mixtures on the market, all of which will work well in this recipe. Or make your own by combining half long-grain brown rice and half wild rice.

If you have fresh thyme on hand, substitute 2 whole sprigs, stem and all, for the dried. Remove and discard before serving.

You can cook the split peas yourself, reserving ¼ cup (50 mL) of the cooking liquid, or you can use 1 can (14 to 19 oz/398 to 540 mL) yellow split peas, rinsed and drained, plus ¼ cup (50 mL) water. Be aware that the canned peas will be much higher in sodium than those you cook yourself.

Poultry, Fish and Meatless Mains

Texas-Style Chicken Stew

This tasty stew, which I adapted from a recipe that appeared in Saveur magazine, is an east Texas tradition. It makes a delicious weekday meal and is perfect for country weekends or tailgate parties. Add crusty rolls and a tossed green salad or coleslaw for a great "down home" meal.

Serves 6

4	slices bacon	4
2	onions, chopped	2
4	cloves garlic, minced	4
1 tsp	dried oregano, crumbled	5 mL
½ tsp	cracked black peppercorns	2 mL
	Salt	
1 cup	chicken stock (store-bought or see recipe, page 135)	250 mL
1	can (14 oz/398 mL) diced tomatoes, with juice	1
3 lbs	skinless bone-in chicken thighs (about 12)	1.5 kg
2	cans (each 14 oz/398 mL) cream-style corn	2
1 tbsp	chili powder, dissolved in 2 tbsp (25 mL) freshly squeezed lemon juice	15 mL
1 tsp	paprika (see tip)	5 mL
Pinch	cayenne pepper (optional)	Pinch

MAKE AHEAD

Complete Steps 1 and 2. Cover and refrigerate for up to 2 days. When you're ready to cook, continue with the recipe.

- **Works best in a large (minimum 5-quart) slow cooker**

1. In a skillet, cook bacon over medium-high heat until crisp. Drain on a paper towel and crumble. Cover and refrigerate until ready to use. Drain off all but 1 tbsp (15 mL) fat from pan.

2. Reduce heat to medium. Add onions to pan and cook, stirring, until softened, about 3 minutes. Add garlic, oregano, peppercorns and salt to taste; cook, stirring, for 1 minute. Add stock and tomatoes with juice; bring to a boil.

3. Arrange chicken over bottom of slow cooker stoneware and cover with vegetable mixture. Cover and cook on Low for 6 hours or on High for 3 hours, until juices run clear when chicken is pierced with a fork. Stir in corn, chili powder solution, paprika, cayenne (if using) and reserved bacon. Cover and cook on High for 30 minutes, until corn is heated through.

TIP

Although any type of paprika, including hot paprika, works well in this recipe, I like to use smoked paprika, which lends a pleasant smoky undertone to the stew.

Caribbean Fish Stew

I love the combination of flavors in this tasty stew. The allspice and the Scotch bonnet peppers add a distinctly island tang. For a distinctive and delicious finish, be sure to include the dill. Serve this with crusty rolls to soak up the sauce, a fresh green salad and some crisp white wine.

Serves 6 to 8

2 tsp	cumin seeds	10 mL
6	whole allspice	6
1 tbsp	olive oil	15 mL
2	onions, finely chopped	2
4	cloves garlic, minced	4
1 tbsp	grated orange or lime zest	15 mL
2 tsp	dried thyme, crumbled	10 mL
1 tsp	ground turmeric	5 mL
½ tsp	cracked black peppercorns	2 mL
2 cups	fish stock	500 mL
1	can (28 oz/796 mL) tomatoes, with juice, coarsely chopped	1
	Salt	
1 to 2	Scotch bonnet peppers, minced	1 to 2
2 cups	sliced okra (¼-inch/ 0.5 cm slices)	500 mL
1½ lbs	skinless grouper fillets, cut into bite-size pieces	750 g
8 oz	shrimp, cooked, peeled and deveined	250 g
½ cup	finely chopped fresh dill (optional)	125 mL

MAKE AHEAD

Complete Steps 1 and 2. Cover and refrigerate for up to 2 days. When you're ready to cook, continue with the recipe.

- **Works in slow cookers from 3½ to 6 quarts**

1. In a large dry skillet over medium heat, toast cumin seeds and allspice, stirring, until fragrant and cumin seeds just begin to brown, about 3 minutes. Immediately transfer to a mortar or a spice grinder and grind. Set aside.

2. In same skillet, heat oil over medium heat for 30 seconds. Add onions and cook, stirring, until softened, about 3 minutes. Add garlic, orange zest, thyme, turmeric, peppercorns and reserved cumin and allspice; cook, stirring, for 1 minute. Add stock and tomatoes with juice; bring to a boil. Season to taste with salt. Transfer to slow cooker stoneware.

3. Cover and cook on Low for 6 hours or on High for 3 hours. Add Scotch bonnet peppers, okra, fish fillets and shrimp. Cover and cook on High for 20 minutes, until fish flakes easily with a fork and okra is tender. Stir in dill (if using).

TIP

One Scotch bonnet pepper is probably enough for most people, but if you're a heat seeker, use two. You can also use habanero peppers instead.

Portuguese Sausage and Shellfish Stew

This robust Portuguese-inspired dish is easy to make, yet produces impressive results. I like to serve this with a big green salad, hot Portuguese cornbread and a crisp white wine.   **Serves 6**

1 lb	fresh chorizo sausage, removed from casings	500 g
4	stalks celery, thinly sliced	4
1	onion, finely chopped	1
4	cloves garlic, minced	4
1 tsp	saffron threads, soaked in 1 tbsp (15 mL) boiling water (optional)	5 mL
¼ tsp	salt	1 mL
¼ tsp	cracked black peppercorns	1 mL
1	can (14 oz/398 mL) diced tomatoes, with juice	1
2 cups	dry white wine	500 mL
½ cup	bottled clam juice	125 mL
½ cup	water	125 mL
1	green bell pepper, finely chopped	1
1 lb	medium shrimp, cooked, shelled and deveined (see tips)	500 g
1 tsp	paprika (see tips)	5 mL
12	mussels or small clams, cleaned (see tips)	12
	Finely chopped fresh parsley	

MAKE AHEAD

Complete Step 1. Cover and refrigerate for up to 2 days. When you're ready to cook, continue with the recipe.

- **Works best in a large (minimum 5-quart) slow cooker**

1. In a nonstick skillet, cook chorizo, celery and onion over medium heat, stirring and breaking meat up with a spoon, until sausage is no longer pink, about 10 minutes. Add garlic, saffron (if using), salt and peppercorns; cook, stirring, for 1 minute. Using a slotted spoon, transfer to slow cooker stoneware.

2. Stir in tomatoes with juice, wine, clam juice and water. Cover and cook on Low for 6 hours or on High for 3 hours, until hot and bubbly. Stir in green pepper, shrimp and paprika. Lay mussels on top and spoon hot liquid over them. (If using clams, see tip, below.) Cover and cook on High for 20 minutes, until mussels have opened. Discard any mussels that do not open.

3. Ladle into large bowls and garnish with parsley.

TIPS

I like to use smoked paprika when making this recipe.

To prepare shrimp for this recipe: In a large pot of boiling salted water, immerse shrimp, in shells. Cook over high heat until shells turn pink, 2 to 3 minutes. Drain and let cool, then peel and devein.

Farmed mussels are preferred for this recipe, as they are very clean and need only to be thoroughly rinsed under cold running water before being cooked. Fresh mussels should be tightly closed, or they should close when you tap them. If not, discard before cooking.

If using fresh clams in this recipe, clean first by scrubbing thoroughly with a wire brush and soaking in several changes of cold salted water. Discard any clams that are open. In a large saucepan over medium-high heat, bring ½ cup (125 mL) cooking liquid from stew to a rapid boil. Add clams, cover and cook, shaking the pot, until all the clams open. Discard any that do not open. Return clams, with liquid, to stew. Garnish and serve.

If desired, substitute 2 cans (each 5 oz/142 g) baby clams, drained and rinsed, for the fresh clams.

Easy Vegetable Chili

Not only is this chili easy to make, it is also delicious. The mild dried chiles add interesting flavor, along with a nice bit of heat. Add the jalapeño only if you're a heat seeker. **Serves 4 to 6**

Vegan Friendly

1 tbsp	vegetable oil	15 mL
4	stalks celery, diced	4
2	onions, chopped	2
4	cloves garlic, minced	4
2 tsp	cumin seeds, toasted and ground (see tip, page 94)	10 mL
2 tsp	dried oregano	10 mL
1 tsp	salt	5 mL
1	can (14 oz/398 mL) diced tomatoes, with juice	1
2 cups	canned red kidney beans, drained and rinsed	500 mL
2	dried New Mexico, ancho or guajillo chiles	2
2 cups	boiling water	500 mL
1 cup	coarsely chopped fresh cilantro	250 mL
1 cup	vegetable stock (store-bought or see recipe, page 134), tomato juice or water	250 mL
1	jalapeño pepper, coarsely chopped (optional)	1
1	green bell pepper, chopped	1
2 cups	corn kernels, thawed if frozen	500 mL

MAKE AHEAD

Complete Steps 1 and 3. Cover and refrigerate tomato and chile mixtures separately for up to 2 days. When you're ready to cook, continue with the recipe.

- Works in slow cookers from 3½ to 6 quarts

1. In a skillet, heat oil over medium heat for 30 seconds. Add celery and onions; cook, stirring, until celery is softened, about 5 minutes. Add garlic, cumin, oregano and salt; cook, stirring, for 1 minute. Add tomatoes with juice and bring to a boil. Transfer to slow cooker stoneware.

2. Stir in beans. Cover and cook on Low for 6 to 8 hours or on High for 3 to 4 hours, until hot and bubbly.

3. About an hour before recipe has finished cooking, combine dried chiles and boiling water in a heatproof bowl. Set aside for 30 minutes, weighing chiles down with a cup to ensure they remain submerged. Drain, discarding soaking liquid and stems, and coarsely chop chiles. Transfer to a blender and add cilantro, stock and jalapeño (if using); purée.

4. Add chile mixture to stoneware, along with green pepper and corn, and stir well. Cover and cook on High for 20 minutes, until pepper is tender and mixture is hot and bubbly.

> **TIPS**
> If you prefer, you can use 1 cup (250 mL) dried red kidney beans, soaked, cooked and drained (see Basic Beans, page 133), instead of the canned beans.
>
> Be aware that if you make the chili mixture (Step 3) ahead of time it will lose some of its vibrancy. For best results, complete Step 3 while the chili is cooking or no sooner than the night before you plan to cook.

Two-Bean Turkey Chili

This tasty chili, which has just a hint of heat, is perfect for family get-togethers. Add a tossed green salad, sprinkled with shredded carrots, and whole-grain rolls.   **Serves 6 to 8**

1 tbsp	olive oil	15 mL
4	stalks celery, diced	4
2	onions, finely chopped	2
6	cloves garlic, minced	6
1 tbsp	cumin seeds, toasted and ground (see tips)	15 mL
2 tsp	dried oregano	10 mL
½ tsp	cracked black pepper	2 mL
	Zest of 1 lime	
2 tbsp	fine cornmeal	25 mL
1 cup	chicken or turkey stock	250 mL
1	can (28 oz/796 mL) tomatoes, with juice, coarsely chopped	1
2 lbs	skinless boneless turkey breast, cut into ½-inch (1 cm) cubes	1 kg
2	cans (each 14 to 19 oz/ 398 to 540 mL) pinto beans, drained and rinsed	2
2 cups	frozen sliced green beans	500 mL
1 tbsp	New Mexico or ancho chili powder, dissolved in 2 tbsp (25 mL) lime juice	15 mL
1	green bell pepper, diced	1
1	red bell pepper, diced	1
1	can (4½ oz/127 mL) diced mild green chiles	1
1	jalapeño pepper or chipotle pepper in adobo sauce, diced (optional)	1

MAKE AHEAD

Complete Step 1. Cover and refrigerate for up to 2 days. When you're ready to cook, continue with the recipe.

- **Works in slow cookers from 3½ to 6 quarts**

1. In a skillet, heat oil over medium heat for 30 seconds. Add celery and onions; cook, stirring, until celery is softened, about 5 minutes. Add garlic and cook, stirring, for 1 minute. Add cumin, oregano, pepper and lime zest; cook, stirring, for 1 minute. Add cornmeal and toss to coat. Add stock and cook, stirring, until mixture boils, about 1 minute. Add tomatoes with juice and return to a boil. Transfer to slow cooker stoneware.

2. Stir in turkey, pinto beans and green beans. Cover and cook on Low for 8 hours or on High for 4 hours, until turkey is tender and mixture is bubbly. Add chili powder solution, green and red peppers, mild green chiles and jalapeño (if using). Cover and cook on High for 30 minutes, until bell peppers are tender.

TIPS

You'll need about 3 cups (750 mL) cubed turkey breast to make this chili.

You can also use leftover turkey. Use 3 cups (750 mL) shredded cooked turkey and add along with the bell peppers.

Add the jalapeño pepper if you're a heat seeker; add the chipotle in adobo sauce if you like a hint of smoke as well.

Toasting the cumin seeds intensifies their flavor. Stir the seeds in a dry skillet over medium heat until fragrant, about 3 minutes. Transfer to a mortar or spice grinder and grind.

Not-Too-Corny Turkey Chili with Sausage

Loaded with vegetables and the complex flavors of a variety of hot peppers, this yummy chili is mild enough to be enjoyed by all family members, even with the addition of a chipotle pepper in adobo sauce.

Serves 6 to 8

1 tbsp	vegetable oil	15 mL
1 lb	mild Italian sausage, removed from casings	500 g
4	stalks celery, diced	4
2	onions, finely chopped	2
6	cloves garlic, minced	6
1 tbsp	cumin seeds, toasted and ground (see tips)	15 mL
1 tbsp	dried oregano	15 mL
1 tsp	salt	5 mL
1	can (28 oz/796 mL) diced tomatoes, with juice	1
1 lb	boneless skinless turkey, cut into ½-inch (1 cm) cubes	500 g
2 cups	canned pinto beans, drained and rinsed	500 mL
2	dried ancho, guajillo or New Mexico chiles	2
2 cups	boiling water	500 mL
1 cup	coarsely chopped fresh cilantro	250 mL
½ cup	chicken stock (store-bought or see recipe, page 135)	125 mL
2 tsp	chili powder	10 mL
1	chipotle chile in adobo sauce (optional)	1
1	red bell pepper, diced	1
2 cups	corn kernels, thawed if frozen	500 mL

MAKE AHEAD

See page 92, including tip.

- **Works best in a large (minimum 5-quart) slow cooker**

1. In a skillet, heat oil over medium heat for 30 seconds. Add sausage, celery and onions; cook, stirring and breaking meat up with a spoon, until sausage is no longer pink, about 10 minutes. Add garlic, cumin, oregano and salt; cook, stirring, for 1 minute. Add tomatoes with juice and bring to a boil. Transfer to slow cooker stoneware.

2. Stir in turkey and beans. Cover and cook on Low for 6 hours or on High for 3 hours, until turkey is no longer pink inside.

3. About an hour before recipe has finished cooking, combine dried chiles and boiling water in a heatproof bowl. Set aside for 30 minutes, weighing chiles down with a cup to ensure they remain submerged. Drain, discarding soaking liquid and stems, and coarsely chop chiles. Transfer to a blender and add cilantro, stock, chili powder and chipotle pepper (if using); purée.

4. Add chile mixture to stoneware, along with red pepper and corn, and stir well. Cover and cook on High for 30 minutes, until pepper is tender and flavors meld.

TIPS

If you prefer, you can use 1 cup (250 mL) dried pinto beans, soaked, cooked and drained (see Basic Beans, page 133), instead of the canned beans.

Toasting the cumin seeds intensifies their flavor. Stir the seeds in a dry skillet over medium heat until fragrant, about 3 minutes. Transfer to a mortar or spice grinder and grind.

Barley Jambalaya

This is a great dish for a family dinner or a casual evening with friends. The robust flavors of the Italian sausage, peppers and Cajun seasonings are delicious at any time of the year, but are particularly appreciated on a chilly night. All you need to add is warm whole-grain rolls, a big salad and, if you're feeling festive, some robust red wine.

Serves 6

1 lb	boneless skinless chicken thighs (about 4), cut into bite-size pieces	500 g
1 tbsp	olive oil	15 mL
8 oz	Italian sausage, removed from casings	250 g
2	onions, finely chopped	2
2	stalks celery, diced	2
4	cloves garlic, minced	4
2 tsp	Cajun seasoning (see tips)	10 mL
1 tsp	dried thyme	5 mL
¾ cup	barley (see tips), rinsed and drained	175 mL
2 cups	chicken stock (store-bought or see recipe, page 135)	500 mL
1	can (28 oz/796 mL) diced tomatoes, with juice	1
2	roasted red bell peppers, cut into strips and diced	2
1	chile pepper, seeded and diced (optional, see tips)	1
8 oz	medium shrimp, cooked, peeled and deveined (optional)	250 g

MAKE AHEAD

Complete Steps 2 and 3, chilling sausage and vegetable mixtures separately. Cover and refrigerate for up to 2 days. When you're ready to cook, continue with the recipe.

- **Works best in a large (minimum 5-quart) slow cooker**

1. Arrange chicken over bottom of slow cooker stoneware.

2. In a large skillet, heat oil over medium–high heat for 30 seconds. Add sausage and cook, stirring and breaking up with a spoon, until no longer pink, about 4 minutes. Drain off all but 1 tbsp (15 mL) fat from pan, if necessary.

3. Reduce heat to medium. Add onions and celery to pan and cook, stirring, until softened, about 5 minutes. Add garlic, Cajun seasoning and thyme; cook, stirring, for 1 minute. Add barley and toss to coat. Add stock and tomatoes with juice; bring to a boil. Transfer to stoneware.

4. Cover and cook on Low for 6 hours or on High for 3 hours, until juices run clear when chicken is pierced with a fork. Add roasted red peppers, chile pepper (if using) and shrimp (if using). Cover and cook on High for about 15 minutes, until heated through.

TIPS

If you don't have Cajun seasoning, substitute 1 tsp (5 mL) of any variety of paprika — sweet, hot or smoked, depending on your taste.

Use the variety of barley you prefer — pearled, pot or whole. Whole (also known as hulled) barley is the most nutritious form of the grain.

If you like heat, add an additional chile pepper. Jalapeño, long red or green or even Thai chiles will work well in this recipe. If you're using a Scotch bonnet or habanero pepper, reduce the quantity to ½ pepper.

Indian-Spiced Chicken and Barley

This is a great dish for Sunday dinner. It is quite easy to make, and the lightly spiced sauce is delectable.

Serves 6

3 lbs	skinless bone-in chicken thighs (about 12)	1.5 kg
3 tbsp	freshly squeezed lemon juice	45 mL
1 tsp	ground turmeric	5 mL
1 tbsp	olive oil	15 mL
4	stalks celery, diced	4
2	onions, finely chopped	2
4	cloves garlic, minced	4
1 tbsp	minced gingerroot	15 mL
1 tbsp	ground cumin (see tips)	15 mL
2 tsp	ground coriander	10 mL
½ tsp	ground cardamom	2 mL
½ tsp	salt	2 mL
1 cup	barley (see tips), rinsed and drained	250 mL
1 cup	chicken stock (store-bought or see recipe, page 135)	250 mL
1	can (28 oz/796 mL) diced tomatoes, with juice	1
1	long red or green chile pepper, finely chopped (or ½ tsp/ 2 mL cayenne pepper)	1
1 cup	full-fat plain yogurt	250 mL

MAKE AHEAD

Complete Steps 1 and 2. Cover and refrigerate chicken and vegetable mixtures separately for up to 2 days. When you're ready to cook, continue with the recipe.

- **Works best in a large (minimum 5-quart) slow cooker**

1. Sprinkle chicken evenly with lemon juice and turmeric; arrange over bottom of slow cooker stoneware.

2. In a skillet, heat oil over medium heat for 30 seconds. Add celery and onions; cook, stirring, until celery is softened, about 5 minutes. Add garlic and ginger; cook, stirring, for 1 minute. Add cumin, coriander, cardamom and salt; cook, stirring, for 1 minute. Add barley and toss to coat. Add stock and tomatoes with juice; bring to a rapid boil. Spread over chicken in stoneware.

3. Cover and cook on Low for 6 hours or on High for 3 hours, until juices run clear when chicken is pierced with a fork.

4. In a small bowl, combine chile pepper and yogurt. Stir into stoneware. Cover and cook on High for 20 minutes, until flavors meld.

TIPS

For the best flavor, toast and grind whole cumin, coriander and cardamom seeds rather than buying the ground versions. Simply stir seeds in a dry skillet over medium heat until fragrant, about 3 minutes. Immediately transfer to a spice grinder or mortar and grind.

Use the variety of barley you prefer — pearled, pot or whole. Whole (also known as hulled) barley is the most nutritious form of the grain. You could also make this dish using an equal quantity of wheat, spelt or Kamut berries.

Arroz con Pollo

This Spanish approach to chicken and rice is a great one-dish meal, delicious enough to serve to guests. I love this version, which has quite a bit of liquid, because I enjoy spooning the luscious sauce over the chicken as I eat and soaking it up with some rustic whole-grain bread. In addition to warm bread, a tossed green salad is all you need.

Serves 6

1 tbsp	olive oil	15 mL
4 oz	fresh chorizo sausage (see tips), removed from casings	125 g
4	cloves garlic, minced	4
2	onions, finely chopped	2
½ tsp	salt (or to taste)	2 mL
½ tsp	cracked black pepper	2 mL
1 cup	long-grain brown rice, rinsed and drained	250 mL
½ cup	dry white wine	125 mL
¼ tsp	crumbled saffron threads, dissolved in 2 tbsp (25 mL) boiling water	1 mL
2 cups	chicken stock (store-bought or see recipe, page 135)	500 mL
1	can (14 oz/398 mL) diced tomatoes, with juice	1
3 lbs	skinless bone-in chicken thighs (about 12)	1.5 kg
1	red bell pepper, diced	1
1 cup	green peas, thawed if frozen	250 mL
2 tsp	sweet paprika (see tips)	10 mL

MAKE AHEAD

Complete Steps 1 and 2, chilling sausage and vegetable mixtures separately. Cover and refrigerate overnight. When you're ready to cook, continue with the recipe.

• **Works best in a large (minimum 5-quart) slow cooker**

1. In a skillet, heat oil over medium–high heat for 30 seconds. Add chorizo and cook, stirring and breaking up with a spoon, until no longer pink, about 2 minutes. Using a slotted spoon, transfer to a plate. Drain off all but 1 tbsp (15 mL) fat from pan.

2. Reduce heat to medium. Add garlic and onions to pan and cook, stirring, until softened, about 3 minutes. Add salt and pepper; cook, stirring, for 1 minute. Add rice and cook, stirring, for 1 minute. Add white wine and saffron mixture; bring to a boil and cook for 1 minute. Add stock and tomatoes with juice; bring to a boil and cook for 2 minutes. Return sausage to pan.

3. Arrange chicken over bottom of slow cooker stoneware and cover with sausage mixture. Place a clean tea towel, folded in half (so you will have two layers), over top of stoneware, to absorb the moisture. (Accumulated moisture affects the consistency of the rice. The tea towel will absorb the moisture generated during cooking.) Cover and cook on Low for 6 hours or on High for 3 hours, until juices run clear when chicken is pierced with a fork. Stir in red pepper, peas and paprika. Cover and cook on High for 20 minutes, until pepper is tender.

TIPS

Chorizo provides the best flavor in this dish, but if you can't find it, Italian sausage makes an acceptable substitute.

If you prefer, substitute hot or smoked paprika for the sweet version. The smoked version will add nice flavor, particularly if you're using Italian sausage rather than chorizo.

Peas and Greens

This delicious combination of black-eyed peas and greens is a great dish for busy weeknights. It also makes a wonderful side dish for roasted meat, particularly lamb.   **Serves 4**

Vegan Friendly

1 tbsp	vegetable oil	15 mL
2	onions, finely chopped	2
1	bulb fennel, cored and thinly sliced on the vertical	1
4	cloves garlic, minced	4
½ tsp	salt (or to taste)	2 mL
½ tsp	cracked black peppercorns	2 mL
¼ tsp	fennel seeds, toasted and ground (see tips)	1 mL
1	can (14 oz/398 mL) diced tomatoes, with juice	1
2 cups	canned black-eyed peas, drained and rinsed	500 mL
1 tsp	paprika (see tips) dissolved in 2 tbsp (25 mL) freshly squeezed lemon juice	5 mL
4 cups	chopped spinach or Swiss chard (about 1 bunch), stems removed	1 L

MAKE AHEAD

Complete Step 1. Cover and refrigerate for up to 2 days. When you're ready to cook, continue with the recipe.

- Works in slow cookers from 3½ to 6 quarts

1. In a skillet, heat oil over medium heat for 30 seconds. Add onions and fennel; cook, stirring, until fennel is softened, about 5 minutes. Add garlic, salt, peppercorns and fennel; cook, stirring, for 1 minute. Add tomatoes with juice and bring to a boil. Transfer to slow cooker stoneware.

2. Stir in peas. Cover and cook on Low for 8 hours or on High for 4 hours, until peas are tender. Stir in paprika solution. Add spinach, stirring until submerged. Cover and cook on High for 20 minutes, until spinach is tender.

TIPS

If you prefer, you can use 1 cup (250 mL) dried black-eyed peas, soaked, cooked and drained (see Basic Beans, page 133), instead of the canned peas.

To prepare fennel, before removing the core, chop off the top shoots (which resemble celery) and discard. If desired, save the feathery green fronds to use as a garnish. If the outer sections of the bulb seem old and dry, peel them with a vegetable peeler before using.

You can use any kind of paprika in this recipe: Regular; hot, which produces a nicely peppery version; or smoked, which adds a delicious note of smokiness. If you have regular paprika and would like a bit a heat, dissolve ¼ tsp (1 mL) cayenne pepper in the lemon juice along with the paprika.

Toasting fennel seeds intensifies their flavor. To toast fennel seeds, stir them in a dry skillet over medium heat until fragrant, about 3 minutes. Transfer to a mortar or spice grinder and grind.

Potato and Pea Coconut Curry

Sweet and white potatoes, cooked in an aromatic sauce, make a simple but very tasty combination. If you have time, substituting Crispy Onion Topping or Crispy Shallot Topping (see page 132) for the cilantro garnish will add delicious flavor and texture to the dish. Serve with warm naan or over hot rice.

Serves 6

Vegan Friendly

1 tbsp	vegetable oil	15 mL
2	onions, finely chopped	2
4	cloves garlic, minced	4
1 tbsp	minced gingerroot	15 mL
½ tsp	cracked black peppercorns	2 mL
1 cup	vegetable stock (store-bought or see recipe, page 134)	250 mL
2	large sweet potatoes (each about 8 oz/250 g), peeled and cut into 1-inch (2.5 cm) cubes	2
2	potatoes, peeled and diced	2
2 tsp	Thai red curry paste (see tips)	10 mL
1 cup	coconut milk, divided	250 mL
2 cups	sweet green peas, thawed if frozen	500 mL
	Finely chopped fresh cilantro	

MAKE AHEAD

Complete Step 1. Cover and refrigerate for up to 2 days. When you're ready to cook, continue with the recipe.

- Works in slow cookers from 3½ to 6 quarts

1. In a skillet, heat oil over medium heat for 30 seconds. Add onions and cook, stirring, until softened, about 3 minutes. Add garlic, ginger and peppercorns; cook, stirring, for 1 minute. Add stock and bring to a boil. Transfer to slow cooker stoneware.

2. Stir in sweet potatoes and potatoes. Cover and cook on Low for 6 to 8 hours or on High for 3 to 4 hours, until potatoes are tender.

3. In a small bowl, combine curry paste and ¼ cup (50 mL) of the coconut milk. Stir until blended. Add to stoneware, along with the remaining coconut milk, and stir well. Stir in peas. Cover and cook on High for 30 minutes, until peas are tender and flavors have melded. When serving, garnish with cilantro.

TIPS

Some curry pastes contain products such as shrimp paste or fish sauce, so if you're a vegetarian, check the label to ensure that yours is fish- and seafood-free.

If you're a heat seeker, you can increase the quantity of curry paste, but this quantity is quite enough for me.

Tagine of Squash and Chickpeas with Mushrooms

I love the unusual combination of flavorings in this dish. The tastes of the cinnamon and ginger really come through, and the bittersweet mixture of lemon and honey, with a sprinkling of currants, adds a perfect finish. Serve this over whole-grain couscous to complement the Middle Eastern flavors. Add a spinach or Swiss chard to complete the meal. **Serves 6**

Vegetarian Friendly

1 tbsp	olive oil	15 mL
2	carrots, peeled and diced (about 1 cup/250 mL)	2
1	onion, finely chopped	1
4	cloves garlic, minced	4
1	stick cinnamon, about 2 inches (5 cm) long	1
2 tbsp	minced gingerroot	25 mL
1 tsp	ground turmeric	5 mL
½ tsp	salt	2 mL
½ tsp	cracked black peppercorns	2 mL
8 oz	cremini mushrooms, stemmed and halved	250 g
1	can (28 oz/796 mL) tomatoes, with juice, coarsely chopped	1
3 cups	cubed butternut squash or pumpkin (1-inch/2.5 cm cubes)	750 mL
2 cups	canned chickpeas, drained and rinsed	500 mL
1 tbsp	liquid honey	15 mL
1 tbsp	freshly squeezed lemon juice	15 mL
¼ cup	currants (optional)	50 mL

MAKE AHEAD

Complete Step 1. Cover and refrigerate for up to 2 days. When you're ready to cook, continue with the recipe.

• **Works in slow cookers from 3½ to 6 quarts**

1. In a large skillet, heat oil over medium heat for 30 seconds. Add carrots and onion; cook, stirring, until carrots are softened, about 7 minutes. Add garlic, cinnamon stick, ginger, turmeric, salt and peppercorns; cook, stirring, for 1 minute. Add mushrooms and toss to coat. Add tomatoes with juice and bring to a boil. Transfer to slow cooker stoneware.

2. Stir in squash and chickpeas. Cover and cook on Low for 8 hours or on High for 4 hours, until vegetables are tender. Discard cinnamon stick.

3. In a small bowl, combine honey and lemon juice. Add to slow cooker and stir well. When serving, sprinkle with currants (if using).

TIPS

I prefer a strong gingery flavor in this dish. If you're ginger-averse, reduce the amount.

If you prefer, you can use 1 cup (250 mL) dried chickpeas, soaked, cooked and drained (see Basic Beans, page 133), instead of the canned chickpeas.

Greek Bean Sauce with Feta

This lip-smacking sauce is particularly delicious as a topping for polenta, but it also works well with brown rice and pasta, particularly orzo. If serving it with pasta, use a whole wheat version or boost the nutritional content by adding bulgur (see variation, below).

Serves 4 to 6

Vegetarian Friendly

1 tbsp	olive oil	15 mL
2	onions, finely chopped	2
2	cloves garlic, minced	2
1	stick cinnamon, about 1 inch (2.5 cm) long	1
1 tsp	dried oregano, crumbled	5 mL
1 tsp	salt	5 mL
½ tsp	cracked black peppercorns	2 mL
1	can (28 oz/796 mL) tomatoes, with juice, coarsely crushed	1
3 cups	frozen sliced green beans	750 mL
½ cup	crumbled feta cheese	125 mL
¼ cup	finely chopped fresh dill	50 mL

VARIATION

Greek Bean Sauce with Bulgur

If you're serving this sauce with pasta, you can boost the nutritional content by stirring in 2 cups (500 mL) soaked bulgur before adding the feta and dill.

MAKE AHEAD

Complete Step 1. Cover and refrigerate for up to 2 days. When you're ready to cook, continue with the recipe.

• **Works in slow cookers from 3½ to 6 quarts**

1. In a large skillet, heat oil over medium heat for 30 seconds. Add onions and cook, stirring, until softened, about 3 minutes. Add garlic, cinnamon stick, oregano, salt and peppercorns; cook, stirring, for 1 minute. Add tomatoes with juice, stirring and breaking up with a spoon. Transfer to slow cooker stoneware.

2. Stir in beans. Cover and cook on Low for 6 hours or on High for 3 hours, until hot and bubbly. Discard cinnamon stick. When serving, sprinkle with feta and dill.

Desserts

The Ultimate Baked Apples

These luscious apples, simple to make yet delicious, are the definitive autumn dessert. I like to serve these with a dollop of whipped cream, but they are equally delicious, and healthier, accompanied by yogurt or on their own.

Serves 8

½ cup	chopped toasted walnuts (see tips)	125 mL
½ cup	dried cranberries	125 mL
2 tbsp	packed muscovado or evaporated cane juice sugar (see tips)	25 mL
1 tsp	grated orange zest	5 mL
8	apples, cored	8
1 cup	cranberry juice	250 mL
	Vanilla-flavored yogurt or whipped cream (optional)	

- **Works best in a large (minimum 5-quart) oval slow cooker**

1. In a bowl, combine walnuts, cranberries, sugar and orange zest. To stuff the apples, hold your hand over the bottom of the apple and, using your fingers, tightly pack core space with filling. One at a time, place filled apples in slow cooker stoneware. Drizzle cranberry juice evenly over tops.

2. Cover and cook on Low for 8 hours or on High for 4 hours, until apples are tender.

3. Transfer apples to a serving dish and spoon cooking juices over them. Serve hot with a dollop of yogurt or whipped cream, if desired.

TIPS

When buying nuts, be sure to source them from a purveyor with high turnover. Because nuts are high in fat (but healthy fat), they tend to become rancid very quickly. This is especially true of walnuts. In my experience, the vast majority of walnuts sold in supermarkets have already passed their peak. Taste before you buy. If they are not sweet, substitute an equal quantity of pecans.

I like the rich molasses taste and the more favorable nutritional profile of muscovado sugar, but light or dark brown sugar makes an acceptable substitute in this recipe.

Oranges in Cointreau

This delightfully different dessert is so easy to make, yet sumptuous enough to satisfy even the most sophisticated palate. It's delicious topped with whipped cream, but I love to serve it as an oh-so-chic sundae, over vanilla ice cream or a complementary sorbet. Yum!   **Serves 8**

1 cup	granulated sugar, divided	250 mL
6	oranges (preferably organic), cut into ¼-inch (0.5 cm) slices, seeds removed	6
1	stick cinnamon, about 2 inches (5 cm) long	1
2 tbsp	Cointreau (see tip)	25 mL

- **Works in slow cookers from 3½ to 6 quarts**

1. Sprinkle ¼ cup (50 mL) of the sugar over the bottom of slow cooker stoneware. Arrange the orange slices on top in overlapping layers, burying the cinnamon stick in the center. Sprinkle the remaining sugar evenly over the oranges. Place a clean tea towel, folded in half (so you will have two layers), over top of stoneware. Cover and cook on High for 4 hours, until the liquid is syrupy and the fruit is soft. Stir in Cointreau.

> **TIP**
> If you prefer, substitute an equal quantity of any other orange-flavored liqueur, such as Triple Sec or Grand Marnier, for the Cointreau.

Blackberry Peach Cobbler

This recipe is an adaptation of one that appeared in Gourmet magazine. It's an absolutely mouth-watering dessert for late summer, when these luscious fruits are at their peak. The advantage of making it in the slow cooker, rather than in the oven, is that you can be doing other things while it cooks to perfection.

Serves 6

4	peaches, peeled and sliced (see tip)	4
3 cups	blackberries (see tip)	750 mL
¾ cup	granulated sugar	175 mL
1 tbsp	cornstarch	15 mL
1 tbsp	freshly squeezed lemon juice	15 mL

TOPPING

1½ cups	all-purpose flour	375 mL
2 tsp	baking powder	10 mL
1 tsp	grated lemon zest	5 mL
½ tsp	salt	2 mL
½ cup	cold butter, cut into 1-inch (2.5 cm) cubes	125 mL
½ cup	milk	125 mL

- Works best in a small (3½-quart) slow cooker
- Lightly greased slow cooker stoneware

1. In prepared stoneware, combine peaches, blackberries, sugar, cornstarch and lemon juice. Stir well. Cover and cook on Low for 4 hours or on High for 2 hours.

2. *Topping:* In a bowl, combine flour, baking powder, lemon zest and salt. Using your fingers or a pastry blender, cut in butter until mixture resembles coarse crumbs. Drizzle with milk and stir with a fork until a batter forms.

3. Drop batter by spoonfuls over hot fruit. Cover and cook on High for 1 hour, until a toothpick inserted in the center comes out clean.

TIP

If you're making this when fresh fruit is out of season, you can substitute 2 cans (each 14 oz/398 mL) sliced peaches, drained, for the fresh and use an equal quantity of frozen blackberries, thawed.

Cranberry Pear Brown Betty

I love the combination of textures and flavors in this old-fashioned favorite. When cranberries are in season, I always freeze a bag or two so I can make this wholesome dessert year-round. It's a great way to use up day-old bread.

Serves 6 to 8

2 cups	dry whole wheat bread crumbs (see tips)	500 mL
2 tbsp	butter, melted, or extra-virgin olive oil	25 mL
6	pears, peeled, cored and sliced	6
1 cup	fresh or frozen cranberries	250 mL
2 tbsp	stevia extract (see tips)	25 mL
1 tbsp	freshly squeezed lemon juice	15 mL
½ cup	cranberry juice	125 mL

- Works best in a small (3½-quart) slow cooker
- Greased slow cooker stoneware

1. In a bowl, combine bread crumbs and butter. Set aside.

2. In a separate bowl, combine pears, cranberries, stevia and lemon juice.

3. Spread one-third of the bread crumb mixture in prepared stoneware. Layer half the pear mixture over top. Repeat. Finish with a layer of crumbs and pour cranberry juice over top. Cover and cook on High for 4 hours, until fruit is tender and mixture is hot and bubbly.

TIPS

To make dry bread crumbs for this recipe, toast 4 slices of whole wheat bread. Tear into pieces and process in a food processor fitted with a metal blade until finely ground.

Use a light whole wheat loaf for this recipe. Those with a heavy molasses content will overpower the fruit.

Stevia is an herb that is almost 300 times sweeter than ordinary sugar and contains virtually no calories. It is used extensively as a sweetener in Japan. If you don't have it, use ¼ cup (50 mL) brown sugar (such as Demerara) or evaporated cane juice sugar (such as Sucanat) instead.

Classic Flan

To the French, a flan is a fruit tart, often including a custard base, but I've always thought the Spanish laid claim to the term with their rich, cold custards surrounded by bittersweet caramel. This version is simple to make and wonderful to eat.

Serves 6

1¾ cups	granulated sugar, divided	425 mL
¼ cup	water	50 mL
1 cup	table (18%) cream	250 mL
1	strip orange or lemon zest	1
1	stick cinnamon, about 2 inches (5 cm) long	1
1 tsp	vanilla	5 mL
3	eggs	3
2	egg yolks	2
	Boiling water	
	Orange slices (optional)	

- Works in a large (minimum 5-quart) oval slow cooker
- Lightly greased 4-cup (1 L) baking dish

1. In a saucepan over medium heat, combine 1 cup (250 mL) of the sugar and the water. Cook, stirring constantly, until sugar is dissolved and mixture comes to a boil. Stop stirring and continue to cook until golden brown, about 5 minutes. Working quickly, pour into prepared dish, tilting to distribute syrup across the bottom and up the sides.

2. In a clean saucepan over medium heat, combine cream, orange zest, cinnamon stick, vanilla and the remaining sugar. Heat just until it reaches the boiling point, then remove from heat and set aside.

3. In a bowl, whisk eggs and egg yolks until blended. Gradually add hot cream mixture, whisking constantly. Strain through a fine sieve into prepared dish. Cover with foil and secure with string.

4. Place dish in slow cooker stoneware and pour in enough boiling water to come 1 inch (2.5 cm) up the sides of the dish. Cover and cook on High for 3 hours, until a toothpick inserted in the center of the custard comes out clean. Chill thoroughly.

5. To serve, run a sharp knife around the edge of the custard and invert onto a serving plate. Serve cold, garnished with orange slices, if desired.

Buttermilk Lemon Sponge

Here's the perfect dessert: creamy yet light, with just a hint of lemon. As it cooks, the egg whites separate into a "sponge" layer, leaving a velvety version of lemon curd on the bottom. Serve this warm, with a mound of fresh berries on the side. Blueberries, raspberries, strawberries — whatever is in season — make an ideal finish.

Serves 4 to 6

½ cup	granulated sugar	125 mL
2	eggs, separated	2
⅔ cup	buttermilk	150 mL
1 tbsp	finely grated lemon zest	15 mL
3 tbsp	freshly squeezed lemon juice	45 mL
¼ cup	all-purpose flour	50 mL
¼ tsp	salt	1 mL
	Boiling water	

- **Works in a large (minimum 5-quart) oval slow cooker**
- **Greased 4-cup (1 L) baking dish**

1. In a mixing bowl, whisk sugar and egg yolks until smooth. Whisk in buttermilk, lemon zest and lemon juice. Whisk in flour and salt until blended.

2. In a separate bowl, beat egg whites until stiff. Gently fold into lemon mixture to make a smooth batter. Spoon into prepared dish. Cover with foil and secure with string.

3. Place dish in slow cooker stoneware and pour in enough boiling water to come 1 inch (2.5 cm) up the sides of the dish. Cover and cook on High for 2½ hours, until a toothpick inserted in the center of the pudding comes out clean.

Plum Pudding

Here's a lightened-up version of a traditional holiday favorite. Allow a week for the mixed pudding to soak in the refrigerator. I like to serve this warm, with a simple lemon sauce or store-bought lemon curd, but if you're a traditionalist, hard sauce works well too. Don't worry about leftovers. It reheats well and, with a steaming cup of tea, will take the chill off even the most blustery winter day.

Serves 8 to 12

1 cup	seedless raisins	250 mL
½ cup	finely chopped mixed candied fruit	125 mL
2 tbsp	chopped candied orange peel	25 mL
2 tbsp	chopped candied ginger	25 mL
	Finely grated zest of 1 orange	
	Finely grated zest of 1 lemon	
½ cup	brandy or dark rum (approx.)	125 mL
¾ cup	all-purpose flour	175 mL
¾ cup	fine dry white bread crumbs	175 mL
2 tbsp	ground toasted blanched almonds	25 mL
1 tsp	ground cinnamon	5 mL
¾ tsp	baking powder	4 mL
¼ tsp	freshly grated nutmeg	1 mL
¼ tsp	salt	1 mL
¾ cup	packed brown sugar	175 mL
½ cup	butter, softened	125 mL
2	eggs	2
2 tbsp	mild-flavored or fancy molasses	25 mL
	Boiling water	

- Works in a large (minimum 5-quart) oval slow cooker
- Lightly greased 6-cup (1.5 L) pudding basin, baking dish or soufflé dish

1. In a bowl, combine raisins, candied fruit, orange peel, candied ginger and orange and lemon zests. Add brandy and stir well. Set aside for 1 hour.

2. In a separate bowl, mix together flour, bread crumbs, ground almonds, cinnamon, baking powder, nutmeg and salt. Set aside.

3. In a clean bowl, beat brown sugar and butter until creamy. Beat in eggs and molasses until incorporated. Stir in soaked fruit mixture. Add flour mixture and mix just until blended. Spoon batter into prepared dish. Cover tightly with plastic wrap and let stand in refrigerator for 1 week, spooning additional brandy over the top two or three times in 1-tbsp (15 mL) increments.

4. Remove plastic wrap. Cover with foil and secure with string. Place dish in slow cooker stoneware and pour in enough boiling water to come 1 inch (2.5 cm) up the sides of the dish. Cover and cook on High for 4 hours, until a toothpick inserted in the center of the pudding comes out clean. Serve hot.

Irish Chocolate Tapioca Pudding

In my opinion, there is nothing quite like tapioca pudding to conjure up memories of motherly love. This version of that old favorite is delicious comfort food with a kick. Serve it with simple wafers, topped with a dollop of whipped cream, and expect requests for seconds. It doesn't get better than this.

Serves 6

¼ cup	tapioca pearls	50 mL
2½ cups	milk, divided	625 mL
6 oz	bittersweet or semisweet chocolate, broken into pieces	175 g
2	eggs	2
½ cup	granulated sugar	125 mL
¼ cup	Irish cream liqueur	50 mL
½ tsp	vanilla	2 mL
	Boiling water	
	Whipped cream	

- Works in a large (minimum 5-quart) oval slow cooker
- Lightly greased 6-cup (1.5 L) baking dish

1. In a bowl, combine tapioca pearls with water to cover. Stir well and set aside for 20 minutes. Drain, discarding liquid. Transfer to prepared dish.

2. Meanwhile, in a saucepan, heat 1 cup (250 mL) of the milk over low heat just until simmering. (Do not boil.) Remove from heat. Add chocolate and stir until melted. Pour into prepared dish and stir to combine.

3. In a blender, combine eggs, sugar, the remaining milk, liqueur and vanilla. Blend until smooth. Pour into prepared dish and stir well. Cover with foil and secure with string.

4. Place dish in slow cooker stoneware and pour in enough boiling water to come 1 inch (2.5 cm) up the sides of the dish. Cover and cook on High for 2½ to 3 hours, until a toothpick inserted in the center of the pudding comes out clean. Stir well.

5. Serve warm or cover and chill overnight. Top with a dollop of whipped cream.

> **TIP**
> Don't confuse the tapioca pearls called for in this recipe with instant tapioca, which is often sold under the Minute brand. Instant tapioca has been thoroughly precooked and would become unpleasantly mushy if soaked then cooked for a prolonged period of time.

Garnishes and Basics

Crispy Onion Topping

1. Cut 3 onions in half, then cut them vertically into paper-thin slices. In a large skillet, heat 1 tbsp (15 mL) oil or clarified butter over medium-high heat. Add the onion slices and cook, stirring constantly, until they are browned and crispy, about 10 minutes.

Crispy Shallot Topping

1. In a skillet, heat 2 tbsp (25 mL) oil or clarified butter over medium-high heat. Add ½ cup (125 mL) diced shallots and cook, stirring, until they are browned and crispy, about 5 minutes.

Harissa
Makes about ⅓ cup (75 mL)

4	cloves garlic	4
3	reconstituted red chile peppers (see tips)	3
2	reconstituted sun-dried tomatoes	2
1½ tbsp	freshly squeezed lemon juice	22 mL
1 tbsp	sweet paprika	15 mL
2 tsp	toasted caraway seeds (see tips)	10 mL
2 tsp	toasted coriander seeds	10 mL
1 tsp	toasted cumin seeds	5 mL
½ tsp	salt	2 mL
3 tbsp	extra-virgin olive oil	45 mL

1. In a mini-chopper, process garlic, chiles, sun-dried tomatoes, lemon juice, paprika, caraway, coriander, cumin and salt until combined. Add oil and process until smooth and blended. Store, covered, in the refrigerator for up to 1 month, covering the paste with a bit of olive oil every time you use it.

TIPS

To prepare the chiles, remove the stems and combine with 1 cup (250 mL) boiling water in a small bowl. Make sure they are submerged and set aside for 30 minutes, until soft. Drain and coarsely chop.

To toast the seeds, combine caraway, coriander and cumin seeds in a dry skillet over medium heat. Cook, stirring, until fragrant, about 3 minutes. Immediately transfer to a spice grinder or mortar and grind.

Basic Beans

Loaded with nutrition and high in fiber, dried beans are one of our most healthful edibles. And the slow cooker excels at transforming them into potentially sublime fare. It is also extraordinarily convenient: Put presoaked beans into the slow cooker before you go to bed, and in the morning they are ready for whatever recipe you intend to make.

Makes about 2 cups (500 mL) cooked beans, about 4 servings

Vegan Friendly

1 cup	dried beans	250 mL
3 cups	water	750 mL
	Garlic, bay leaves or bouquet garni (optional)	

DRIED LENTILS

These instructions also work for lentils, with the following changes: Do not presoak them and reduce the cooking time to about 6 hours on Low.

- **Works in slow cookers from 3½ to 6 quarts, depending on quantity of beans**

1. *Long soak:* In a bowl, combine beans and water. Soak for at least 6 hours or overnight. Drain and rinse thoroughly with cold water. Beans are now ready to cook.

2. *Quick soak:* In a pot, combine beans and water. Cover and bring to a boil. Boil for 3 minutes. Turn off heat and soak for 1 hour. Drain and rinse thoroughly with cold water. Beans are now ready to cook.

3. *Cooking:* In slow cooker stoneware, combine 1 cup (250 mL) beans, presoaked, and 3 cups (750 mL) fresh cold water. If desired, season with garlic, bay leaves or a bouquet garni made from your favorite herbs tied together in a cheesecloth bag. Cover and cook on Low for 10 to 12 hours or on High for 5 to 6 hours, until beans are tender. Drain and rinse. If not using immediately, cover and refrigerate. The beans are now ready to use in your favorite recipe.

TIPS

This recipe may be doubled or tripled to suit the quantity of beans required for a recipe.

Soybeans and chickpeas take longer to cook than other legumes. They will likely take the full 12 hours on Low (about 6 hours on High).

Once cooked, legumes should be covered and stored in the refrigerator, where they will keep for 4 to 5 days. Cooked legumes can also be frozen in an airtight container for up to 6 months.

Basic Vegetable Stock

One benefit of making your own stock is that you can control the amount of salt you add. This recipe, which makes enough for two average soup recipes, can be made ahead and frozen. For convenience, cook it overnight in the slow cooker. If your slow cooker is not large enough to make a full batch, you can halve the recipe. **Makes about 12 cups (3 L)**

Vegan Friendly

8	carrots, scrubbed	8
6	stalks celery	6
3	onions	3
3	cloves garlic	3
6	sprigs fresh parsley	6
3	bay leaves	3
10	whole black peppercorns	10
1 tsp	dried thyme	5 mL
	Salt (optional)	
12 cups	water	3 L

VARIATIONS

Roasted Vegetable Stock

Preheat oven to 425°F (220°C). In a bowl, toss chopped carrots, celery, onions and garlic in 1 tbsp (15 mL) olive oil. Spread on a baking sheet and roast, turning 3 or 4 times, for 20 minutes, until nicely browned. Transfer to slow cooker stoneware, add remaining ingredients and proceed with recipe.

Enhanced Vegetable Stock

To enhance 8 cups (2 L) Basic Vegetable Stock or prepared stock, combine in a large saucepan over medium heat with 2 carrots, peeled and coarsely chopped, 1 tbsp (15 mL) tomato paste, 1 tsp (5 mL) celery seeds, 1 tsp (5 mL) cracked black peppercorns, ½ tsp (2 mL) dried thyme, 4 sprigs fresh parsley, 1 bay leaf and 1 cup (250 mL) white wine. Bring to a boil. Reduce heat to low, cover and simmer for 30 minutes, then strain and discard solids.

- Works best in a large (minimum 6-quart) slow cooker

1. Coarsely chop carrots, celery, onions and garlic. Place in slow cooker stoneware and combine with parsley, bay leaves, peppercorns, thyme, salt to taste (if using) and water. Cover and cook on Low for 8 hours or on High for 4 hours. Strain and discard solids. Cover and refrigerate for up to 5 days or freeze in an airtight container.

Homemade Chicken Stock

There's nothing quite like the flavor of homemade chicken stock. It's very easy to make — you can cook it overnight, strain it in the morning and refrigerate it during the day. By the time you return home, the fat will have congealed on top of the stock and you can skim it off. This recipe makes enough for two average soup recipes. Use what you need and freeze the remainder for another recipe. If your slow cooker is not large enough to make the full quantity, you can cut the recipe in half.

Makes about 12 cups (3 L)

4 lbs	bone-in skin-on chicken parts	2 kg
4	carrots, scrubbed and coarsely chopped	4
4	stalks celery, coarsely chopped	4
3	onions, coarsely chopped	3
6	sprigs fresh parsley	6
3	bay leaves	3
10	whole black peppercorns	10
1 tsp	dried thyme	5 mL
	Salt (optional)	
12 cups	water	3 L

VARIATIONS

Slow Cooker Turkey Stock

Substitute 1 turkey carcass, broken into pieces, for the chicken parts.

Stovetop Turkey Stock

Break a turkey carcass into manageable pieces and place in a stockpot. Add 2 quartered carrots, 2 quartered celery stalks, 2 quartered onions and 8 whole black peppercorns. Add water to cover and bring to a boil over medium-high heat. Reduce heat to low, cover and simmer for 3 hours, then strain and discard solids.

- Works best in a large (minimum 6-quart) slow cooker

1. In slow cooker stoneware, combine chicken, carrots, celery, onions, parsley, bay leaves, peppercorns, thyme, salt to taste (if using) and water. Cover and cook on High for 8 hours. Strain into a large bowl, discarding solids. Refrigerate liquid until fat forms on surface, about 6 hours. Skim off fat. Cover and refrigerate for up to 5 days or freeze in an airtight container.

TIPS

The more economical parts of the chicken, such as necks, backs and wings, make the best stock.

If you want to use this stock soon after it has finished cooking, strain it into a bowl (preferably stainless steel) and set in a sink filled with ice water, replenishing the ice as necessary, until the stock has cooled to room temperature. Stir well and refrigerate until fat forms on the surface.

Library and Archives Canada Cataloguing in Publication

Finlayson, Judith
　　Sensational slow cooker gourmet / Judith Finlayson.

Includes index.
ISBN-13: 978-0-7788-0199-3.
ISBN-10: 0-7788-0199-3

1. Electric cookery, Slow.　I. Title.

TX827.F558 2008　　　　641.5'884　　　　C2008-902459-1

Index

More Bestsellers by Judith Finlayson

978-0-7788-0038-5 U.S. / 978-0-7788-0041-5 CAN

978-0-7788-0053-8 U.S. / 978-0-7788-0052-1 CAN

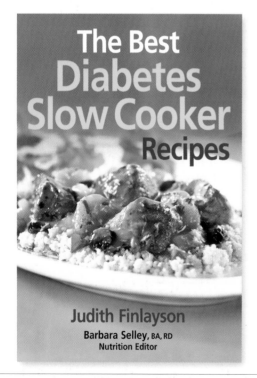

ISBN 978-0-7788-0169-6

ISBN 978-0-7788-0172-6

175 Essential
Slow Cooker
Classics

Judith Finlayson

ISBN 978-0-7788-0143-6

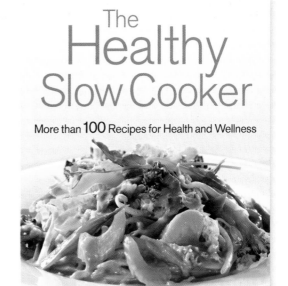

The
Healthy
Slow Cooker

More than 100 Recipes for Health and Wellness

Judith Finlayson

ISBN 978-0-7788-0133-7

125 best
Vegetarian
Slow Cooker
recipes

Judith Finlayson

ISBN 978-0-7788-0104-7

125 best
Rotisserie
Oven recipes

Judith Finlayson

ISBN 978-0-7788-0110-8

Available Wherever Books Are Sold

Also Available

the Complete
Whole Grains
Cookbook

150 Recipes for Healthy Living

Judith Finlayson

ISBN 978-0-7788-0178-8

For more great books, see previous pages